Releasing Your Child's Potential

Inspiring, informative books for thoughtful readers wanting to make changes
and realise their potential.

Other titles in the series include:

Choosing a Better Life
*An inspiring step-by-step guide to
building the future you want*

Picking Winners
*A total hiring system for spotting exceptional performers
and getting them on board*

When What You've Got Is Not What You Want
Use NLP to create the life you want and live it to the full

Getting Your Next Job
A systematic approach to finding the career that is best for you

Please send for a free copy of the catalogue for full details
(see back cover for address).

Releasing
Your Child's Potential

Empower your child to
set and reach their own goals

Sylvia Clare

PATHWAYS

First published in 2000 by
How To Books Ltd, 3 Newtec Place,
Magdalen Road, Oxford OX4 1RE, United Kingdom
Tel: 01865 793806   Fax: 01865 248780

British Library Cataloguing in Publication Data
A catalogue record for this book is available from
the British Library

Edited by Julie Nelson   Cover image PhotoDisc
Cover design by Shireen Nathoo Design
Cover copy by Sallyann Sheridan

Produced for How To Books by Deer Park Productions
Typeset by Anneset, Weston-super-Mare, Somerset
Printed and bound by Hillman Printers, Frome, Somerset

Note: The material contained in this book is set out in good
faith for general guidance and no liability can be accepted for loss or expense
incurred as a result of relying in particular circumstances on statements made in
the book. The laws and regulations are complex and liable to change, and readers
should check the current position with the relevant authorities before making
personal arrangements.

Pathways is an imprint of
How To Books

Contents

Preface

When thinking of children, as a parent or teacher, one of the most enduring images is that of listening to stories. Perhaps you remember special stories that captivated you when you were a child. Stories that wanted you to read them over and over again, until you knew them word perfect. So what was that special something that hooked you so strongly? Stories represent closeness, imagination, shared pleasures, intimacy and much more. But the real power of stories is in what they teach us. The child psychologist Jerome Bruner showed that incidental learning, or unintentional learning, is often that which stays with us the longest. And stories linger in our memories for years, right into adulthood. So we can reclaim our early pleasure when sharing a story with a child. But what is the real power about stories? It is the power to teach us many things, and this has been the basis for stories for hundreds of years, to entertain and to teach. Stories can teach us emotional intelligence, give ideas of how to approach the tricky areas of life in advance, give ideas about what to do and what not to do. We are all learning how to be an improved version of our selves every day. Stories enable this process in a non threatening and non confrontational way. And it takes courage to admit the need to change and then to actively seek to do it.

This book is written with full acknowledgement of all the learning opportunities I have had in my years of teaching and working with young people. They taught me so much, but above all showed me that inside even the most difficult child or teenager, there is a loving and gentle person wanting to be free. They are only waiting for an opportunity to express themselves as they truly are. Yet society labels them as difficult and traps them in an unhappiness, which limits them from revealing who they really are and what they are capable of achieving.

In private practice I have worked with mature adults who were still waiting for their inner child of joy and spontaneity to be released. They have learned the true meaning of peace and have learned to love their inner child.

This book is based on the learning experiences I have shared with all, in an attempt to make the future easier and gentler for everyone. It is aimed at everyone and anyone who works with children, either as a parent or in any other capacity, or anyone who wants to change society and create a more accepting and loving environment for all.

Special thanks go to Matthew and Ben for being my loving, forgiving and very patient teachers as I learned how to be a good parent, and to Cordelia, Morag, Caying and Rachel for the time we shared together. They all helped me to be a better person and showed me the importance of what to write in this book.

CHAPTER 1

Exploring Potential

E ach individual is a unique combination of attributes, traits, skills and talents – the basis and the sum of their **potential**. This is true not only of you as a parent or professional working with children, but also, and most importantly, of your children or the children with whom you work. Each attribute and trait, skill and talent can be:

- used in positive and productive ways
- used in self-limiting and damaging ways
- undervalued or treated as of minor importance
- allowed to lie dormant, and the potential value completely unrecognised.

Ultimately, people with the most successful lives have recognised their attributes and talents and can use them in positive and productive ways for whichever areas of their lives they choose. Often the full positive potential of certain characteristics is not immediately apparent. It is likely, therefore, that some of the world's most successful people had many of the following experiences in common:

- They may not have always performed well at school.
- Perhaps they were perceived as rebellious, difficult or non-conformist children.
- They have their own strong ideas, and may often have been stubborn and refused to do as they were told as children.
- They have a strong sense of self and challenge the 'norm'.
- They are able to bring into play all their attributes as a combined talent.
- They are 'internally referenced', i.e. not all that bothered about what other people think of them.
- They do not need to compare or compete with others, only

with their last performance.

- They are able to be different without being self-conscious or feeling wrong.
- They have the courage and confidence to look at life from different angles and recognise the full range of possibilities that life offers.
- They are not ashamed or discouraged by their mistakes but use them to learn from and develop new approaches or strategies.

So how can we harness these and other characteristics and channel them in such a way as to achieve positive outcomes? This book will suggest some of the ways in which parents can help children to achieve their potential.

> You cannot expect your child to achieve anything if you are not prepared to achieve for yourself as well. Recognising your full emotional potential as a parent is equally important.

Although they all overlap, and there are many more, the areas I will be focusing on are:

- emotional
- intellectual
- social and interpersonal.

These in turn combine to influence our relationships of all kinds, including our relationship with ourself, which is the basis of all our potential.

Developing potential or creating limitations

In order to understand how to maximise the potential in a child, it is equally important to recognise how potential can be blocked. Potential can be either thwarted or developed through:

- the approach to discipline and control of behaviour
- the various forms of example a child is shown
- the kind of encouragement they receive
- their own drive and initiative
- the level of emotional self-awareness and expression they are encouraged to have
- their degree of openness to intuitive and subjective experiences

- their own sense of timing and being ready to perform
- the social structures and expectations in which they are reared
- the beliefs and approaches to life held by influential 'others' in a child's life.

Ironically you will notice that potential can be both liberated and thwarted through the same dimensions of experience. So it is not what we do but how we do it that really matters as parents. Becoming increasingly aware of what we are really doing in our daily lives, both to ourselves as parents and to our children, will enable us to recognise and allow our children to develop their full potential in all areas of life. Parents teach as much by example as by any pro-active intentions and policies. So the way you treat yourself is just as important as the way you treat your child.

Case study: Jane _____

Jane is an interesting child. Her character is challenging, questioning, self-assured and self-directed. She loves to explore and is fascinated by the natural world. She is a solitary child who loves to read and think about life. She likes to go off into her own worlds of imagination and lives with a very rich tapestry of dreams and psychic experiences.

Jane is growing up in a household that does not understand or recognise these attributes. Her family view her as a difficult child. Her parents find these traits hard to cope with. They see her as argumentative, antisocial, selfish and disobedient. In an attempt to control her she is often smacked hard by her father and criticised by her mother. She is informed that she is intelligent, but whatever she puts any effort into, fault is always found, however small. She stops trying and is told she is lazy.

Jane feels that, as she is, she is wrong. She spends most of her childhood trying to become someone else, someone who gets approval and praise. She is told that she is beaten for her own benefit and believes that this is the way parents show love. But she is also becoming increasingly desperate inside. She believes her parents are wrong and hopes she can gain their acceptance and approval. She wants to wake them up to the truth about her, to see an alternative. In adolescence Jane uses her characteristics to provoke and challenge her parents, doing the opposite of whatever they want. Both parents only see the 'problem child' and Jane begins to believe everything she has been told about herself. Her parents must be right after all.

As Jane reaches adulthood she is unable to achieve anything and takes menial jobs because this is all that she feels she is worth. Her parents still criticise whatever she does. Jane is a very angry and confused person inside. She is unable to use her strengths in a positive way. _____

Recognising the positive in everything

In reality an attribute can only ever be neutral. It is the use to which it is put that decides whether it is positive or negative. But when we are being instructed or given feedback about our behaviour in childhood we may be told that it is a bad attribute, as Jane was told that her love of being alone was 'antisocial'. If a character trait is labelled 'bad', we have to ask, 'bad for whom?'

The chances are that if a child is 'difficult' the truth is that the parents are mis-managing the child and cannot cope. There is rarely anything difficult about a child, other than that they may not meet the expectations of the adults around them. So who is 'difficult', the child for being who they are or the adult world for placing impossible expectations on the child?

Try it now   Make a list of all your attributes, etc., however you view them. Make a note of how you use each of them. Make a special note of the ones that you have come to recognise as negative traits or behaviours. Now choose a positive use for each of those attributes. Even so-called negative ones have a positive potential. Spend some time over this and come back to it several times, until you have a fully comprehensive and positive list for yourself. Ask close friends and trusted family members to help you, as it can be hard to recognise our 'self' if we are not used to it. Be as non-judgemental as you can. There are no rights or wrongs, only potentials.

When you have completed this exercise, you might also like to read one of the stories beginning on page 135 that illustrate these points in more detail. Read the story of Violet now.

Adopting realistic expectations

If we want to maximise the potential of a child we must first stop imposing our ideas on them and allow them to show us what they can do. This is the first step to take in changing your attitude. What are your priorities? What are your personal models of potential and success? The chances are, if you are reading this book, that your children are one of your priorities – bringing them up with a good start in life, keeping them safe until they are old enough to be independent. So how are you doing?

It is important to keep in mind that generally there is no right or wrong way to parent. Eighty per cent of parents get it right more or less and each style of parenting teaches your child something. Sometimes the outcome isn't what we expected and this can make it harder for your child to be successful, but that is part of the learning experience for both of you. It is how we address our mistakes that really counts.

Before going any further, we should address the issue of **expectations** and **priorities**. Our expectations and priorities are underpinned by our whole belief system about how life works. Most of us, however, have not really questioned the values we live with, we just accept them as normal.

Try it now

Look at each of the areas listed below. What are the most important areas of your own life? Are there any other priorities that you would want to add? Number the list in order of importance for you, taking time to reflect before you complete this exercise.

(a) relationship with spouse/partner
(b) relationship(s) with child/ren
(c) relationships with friends
(d) relationships at work
(e) success at work
(f) material comfort and status
(g) social image and reputation
(h) feeling at peace with yourself and your conscience
(i) winning or excelling at something
(j) winning approval from other people
(k) other.

Now consider each area in the following way:

◆ How much time and effort do you put into each of the areas, how much thought and planning, how much energy?
◆ What proportion of your waking time do you spend actively in each of these areas of your life?

- Of course, at work you have to think about work, but do you think about other areas of your life during the day?
- Do you find yourself thinking about work when you are at home with your family?
- Are you working for the family or living for your work?

Finally, give a priority score to each of the areas listed, using a 1–5 scale where 1 = high priority and 5 = low priority.

Assessing your scores

It is useful if both you and your co-parent complete this exercise, and if you then compare your perceived priorities and value systems with those of your colleagues, friends and others around you. What does this tell you about your belief system in life? How balanced are the areas of your life? How does your score compare with your partner's? The closer your score compares to your partner's score, the more in tune you are with each other. A good sign for consistency at least, but let's explore a little further.

If you are in tune with each other as parents, you are also likely to be very conscious of your concepts of success. You are likely to choose how to spend your time and energy quite carefully. If your scores differ considerably, where does this occur?

This exercise does not have right or wrong answers. It is simply another way of exploring your present sense of self and your priorities in life – and, with reflection, how this can affect your child.

| Try it now | **Prioritising for children** |

Apply the same assessment procedure for the list below. It is helpful to do a comparison with your co-parent here too. What do you regard as of most importance for your children?

(a) relationships with siblings
(b) relationships with parents
(c) relationships with friends
(d) success at school/college/work
(e) material comfort and status now and in the future
(f) social image and reputation (theirs – and yours through them)
(g) feeling at peace with themselves and their conscience

(h)   winning or excelling at something
(i)   winning approval from other people, especially you as
parents
(j)   other.

Comparing the lists

How do the two lists equate with each other? If your child is old
enough, ask them to complete their own list and compare your
list with your child's. The closer your lists are to each other the
more likely you are to succeed in the parenting/learning process.
If your ideas are different from the ideas and priorities of your
children you could discuss this with them. Do not impose your
ideas on them. Allow them to explain their feelings and choices
and perhaps discuss the reasons for their choices. Suggest there
may be better choices but allow them to re-assess their priorities
in their own time. Keeping them open to their own choices is far
more important than imposing your own values, even if this
seems more risky in the short term.

Understanding our needs

We gradually develop priorities by acknowledging our **needs**.
These include, material and physiological needs for the
maintenance of life, emotional needs, esteem needs, social needs
and intellectual needs.

> A need is a basic requirement of daily life for any individual.
> Until it is met, there is a tension in the experience of life that
> creates discomfort.

Needs vary as much as individuals do, but there are patterns of
need that are common to all of us. Abraham Maslow described
these as a hierarchy, which he represented in two sections, 'Basic'
or 'Deficiency' needs and 'Being' needs (see Figure 1).

It is now argued that the needs are of equal significance, and
that, for instance, we can meet level three and four without level
one being met. Maslow acknowledged that many role models for
his theory of self-actualisation (see page 26) were quite unhappy

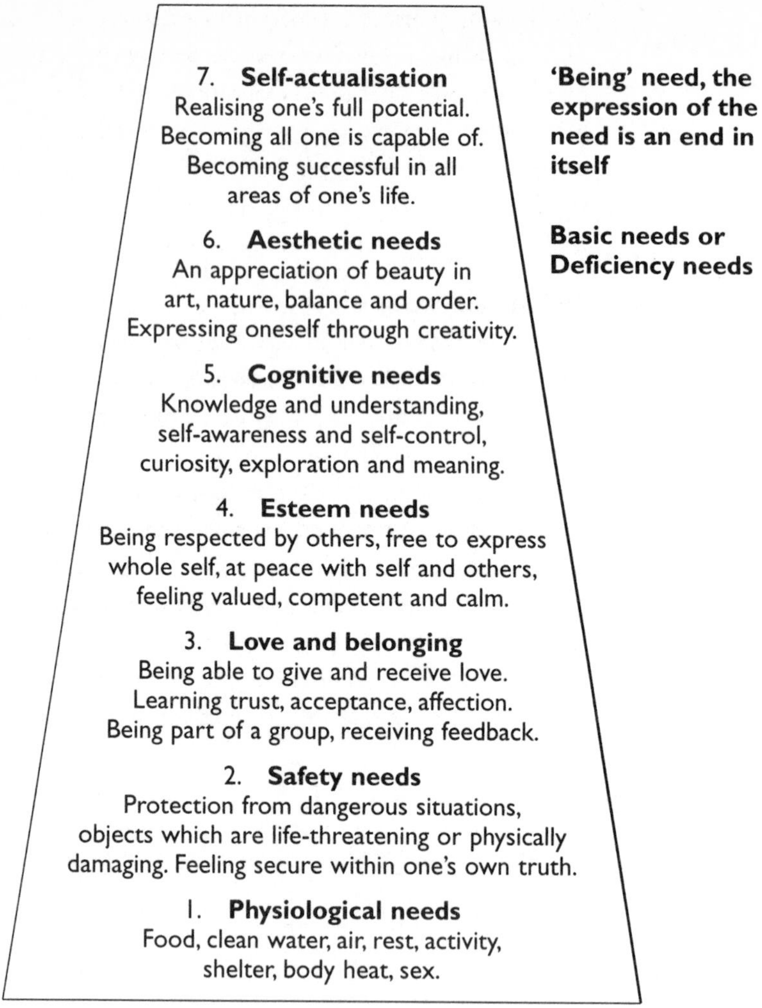

7. **Self-actualisation**
Realising one's full potential.
Becoming all one is capable of.
Becoming successful in all
areas of one's life.

**'Being' need, the
expression of the
need is an end in
itself**

6. **Aesthetic needs**
An appreciation of beauty in
art, nature, balance and order.
Expressing oneself through creativity.

**Basic needs or
Deficiency needs**

5. **Cognitive needs**
Knowledge and understanding,
self-awareness and self-control,
curiosity, exploration and meaning.

4. **Esteem needs**
Being respected by others, free to express
whole self, at peace with self and others,
feeling valued, competent and calm.

3. **Love and belonging**
Being able to give and receive love.
Learning trust, acceptance, affection.
Being part of a group, receiving feedback.

2. **Safety needs**
Protection from dangerous situations,
objects which are life-threatening or physically
damaging. Feeling secure within one's own truth.

1. **Physiological needs**
Food, clean water, air, rest, activity,
shelter, body heat, sex.

Fig. 1. Abraham Maslow's hierarchy of needs.

in other areas of their life. They had to sacrifice one area in order
to achieve in another. But is this necessary? Any emotionally
intelligent adult can actively develop themselves well enough to
achieve and maintain a successful balance in all aspects of their
life, to fully recognise all their potential.

Balancing needs

Although the needs listed in Figure 1 are common to all humans,
it is the balance between each of them that is affected by our
childhood and life experiences. Childhood creates the mould or

structure of reality and experiences are interpreted to confirm this sense of reality. Thus if experience places material needs as a higher order priority than intellectual needs, that will become our priority for adult life in one way or another. Even if it is our priority to challenge this attitude, it is still a priority. Whatever we react to is a priority. Only when we are no longer concerned with it has it become neutral and not a priority in our lives.

Case study: Mike and Mary _____

Mike and Mary have two children, John and Michele, aged four and six. They both work full time and the family live in a spacious home with every comfort. They have an excellent trained nanny and both children attend private prep school. At weekends the whole family go to a sports centre for coaching lessons in a range of sports. After the lessons they all go for a family meal and sit around a table discussing the achievement and progress each has made. The children also have a number of after-school activities such as music lessons, and both children are expected to practise regularly. They are continuously coached to 'get better' at everything. Mike and Mary are very proud of the success of their parenting strategy and, to each other, recognise the competence of each child already. They are reluctant to praise the children too much in case it encourages complacency.

John and Michele work very hard at trying to please their parents. They rarely see them and are often reminded about how hard Mum and Dad both work to provide them with all the good things they have in life. They feel guilty if they cannot show some progress each week as a reward for their parents. They do not enjoy their activities and feel laden with responsibility to succeed. They both feel inadequate because they are unable to meet their parents' high expectations sufficiently to receive the praise which they see their friends receiving from their parents for what seems to be much less. They both already feel that somehow they must be woefully inadequate in ways that neither can understand.

Twenty years on, Mike and Mary tell all their friends how proud they are of both of their children in their academic records and professional achievement. They are hoping that eventually one of them will find a steady partner and settle down and provide them with grandchildren too. At the moment neither seem able to keep a partner for long. There's always something 'wrong' with them. And they are concerned that already John has high blood pressure and Michele has irritable bowel syndrome, both stress-related conditions. Mike feels that they should find a good family life like they had when they were young, in order to cope with the stress and help them to relax. _____

This case study might seem rather exaggerated but it reflects what happens in many families at some level or another. Answering the following questions in relation to the case study will help you recognise your own patterns of priorities and needs. Remember, if you react it reflects something of importance inside you.

- What have John and Michele been taught about themselves and their intrinsic value?
- Was this what their parents intended?
- What did the parents intend to show their children?
- What adjustment could they have made to their parenting style which would have made a difference?
- Which parenting skill are they demonstrating a lack of?
- Both parents identify an area of failure in their children's lives – where do they look for the explanation for this?

Consider your answers to these questions carefully and look for any area of your own parenting skills where you might be falling short. Honestly acknowledge it and forgive yourself for making a mistake, so that you do not make your child more laden with guilt and responsibility for forgiving you and making you feel better. Simply tell your child that you are getting it wrong, and that you will try hard to get it right in the future. They will feel much better for this and will have more respect for you for being honest and human. They will learn that, if you can get things wrong, they are allowed to as well.

Allowing risks

Protecting and channelling your children can mean that inadvertently you do the opposite. If you do all the protecting, how can your children learn to protect themselves? If you choose the direction for your children, how can they learn to make their own choices?

We can control some of their environment and experiences and obviously protect them from life-threatening situations, but the more we try and control life, the more impossible it becomes. Both parent and child then become involved in a major power battle over who is controlling whose life. If you do not allow your child to take risks and face difficult situations, they will generally respond in one of two ways:

- they will either withdraw completely and be quite unable to face anything, or
- they will become high risk-takers, and rebellious, to prove their independence.

Accepting change

Life is a continuous process of change. Our priorities change and grow as the circumstances around us change. The ability to change our priorities in response to the changes around us is an essential life skill. We need to keep a sense of perspective on everything at all times and respond flexibly in order to achieve a balance that brings inner peace and success, the elements of emotional intelligence. Realising potential is a gradual and ongoing process of change for everyone, whatever their age. Childhood is a good place to start but not the only one, as we will see.

Summary

This chapter has introduced several ideas about potential, success and the basic nature of each individual. Children cannot learn to value and utilise their potential if the other people in their lives do not value their own potential and that of the child.

- Emotional self-awareness and intelligence matter as much as individual characteristics.
- Priorities are important to assess for parents and for children.
- Valuing mistakes is an essential part of achieving potential for both parents and children.
- Co-parents can examine and refine their priorities to be more in tune with each other.
- Children should be allowed to develop their own priorities.
- Parents need to remain flexible to the changes in needs and priorities of children through different ages.

CHAPTER 2

Understanding Emotional Competence

E motions are the basis of subjective experience in life. In truth, experience is always neutral, that is, neither good nor bad, but we generally don't feel it as neutral. That is why one person's difficult experience can be someone else's joyful experience. The actual occurrences or events are the same but it is the subjective interpretations that create these judgements or choices. **Emotional intelligence** or **competence** is being able to recognise, use and effectively work with our emotions all the time.

Recognising subjectivity

Our emotions are unique to us. Although we commonly relate to shared emotional experiences, nevertheless there is a difference for all of us in how we interpret and experience our emotions.

1 If the experience bears any connections to our own life, we feel it according to our subjective perception.
2 If it happens to someone else, we empathise, that is, we imagine what we would feel like if we were in the same position.
3 If it is of no importance to our value and belief system, we are unlikely to respond with any emotional intensity.

The strength of our emotional response is a demonstration of the importance of the issue or occurrence in our life.

Emotions are the messengers of experience. They tell us one of the following:

◆ This is a good and enjoyable experience.
◆ This is an unpleasant experience and not to be repeated.
◆ This feels good right now but I might regret it later on.
◆ This is a hard experience but I know I will not regret it later on.
◆ This is a familiar experience and easy to deal with.

♦ This is against my own beliefs and boundaries and feels uncomfortable.

Can you add any more to this list?

The point about messengers is that they can leave once they have delivered their message. Then we can recognise the message we have been given. Holding on to emotions is like putting the messenger in prison – it requires a lot of energy and resources. Holding on to emotions costs us a great deal in emotional and intellectual terms. If we use our resources in this way, we cannot use them to realise our potential.

> Releasing all negative thoughts, feelings and emotions is crucial for anyone to be able to realise their full potential. Holding on to them is creating limitations for oneself.

In order to understand our emotions and use them effectively as messengers, we first have to learn to recognise exactly what they are telling us.

Try it now   Spend one day making a list of all the emotions you experience as you go through. Step back from each experience and ask yourself, 'What am I feeling right here and right now?' What are the physical symptoms? What are the emotions and thoughts telling me?

Now list the emotions and related experiences in two columns: one for joyful emotions and one for difficult emotions. If you have experiences that bring mixed feelings with them, enter the relevant feelings in both columns.

We will come back to this exercise later on. Remember there are no right or wrong answers, simply opportunities to explore your understanding of yourself as you are now and where your potential for growth and change lies.

Identifying emotional variations

Most people are not fully aware of exactly what they are feeling. The tendency is to respond automatically without first considering what they really feel and, more importantly, why. The three stories at the end of this book (see page 135) explore a wide range of emotional experiences. We often relate to stories more easily than to our own direct experience, so use the three stories for yourself firstly and then with your children. They can form the basis for developing an understanding of how our own emotional responses work as adults, and can be directly related to personal experience and used for our children later. Whatever you think you know about your emotional responses, be assured that there are far more layers that you do not yet know. Humans are like icebergs – we often only ever 'see' the part above water and assume that is all there is.

Try is now   If you have not already done so, read the stories beginning on page 135, now. Note your responses to each of the stories as you read them.

1   If you react to the story at all, you are relating the message to yourself personally at some level. The story reflects some aspect of your own experience which you have not yet resolved.
2   If you deny that the message in a story has any relevance to you, you are denying part of the message from your own unconscious and your own life. You are hiding from your messengers, your truth.
3   If you can see and relate to exactly what the story tells you without reacting emotionally, you have reached a stage of self-awareness that is based on chosen responses, not reactions or suppressions. You have learned how to feel *and* how to release.

This third position is a goal for realising potential. However, it is important not to pretend to yourself that this is where you are if it is not the case. There is nothing wrong with where you are, as long as you will allow yourself to develop from this position. Mostly you will find that you have a range of all three of these responses to different aspects of each story. This demonstrates that you have some issues resolved and some not, like everyone else.

Labelling emotions

We are accustomed to a rich vocabulary that describes the range and nuance of our emotional responses to different experiences. We assume the words represent emotions that are different from each other. By analysing the rudiments of each emotion, we find that basically there are only two emotions, **fear** and **joy**. Everything else originates here.

The importance of the emotion is decided by the intensity of physical response. The perception of the cause or source of the emotion tells us it is fear or joy, or any variation of these.

Emotional origins

Both fear and joy originate in a part of the brain called the **limbic system**, which has the ability to identify a source, e.g. a threat, and respond milliseconds before conscious awareness of the danger.

The limbic system has two capacities, memory and learning. The predominant experience in childhood is the predominant emotional experience in adulthood because the limbic system has learned to respond in the biased way according to experience. Our brain can be programmed to experience joy or fear as a dominant response, according to the kind of childhood we have had. As parents we can decide how to programme our child, and as adults we can recognise and modify our own programming.

> It is quite possible to retrain the perceptual basis of your brain from negative to positive, using hypnosis, Neuro Linguistic Programming and similar therapeutic approaches.

Experiencing fear positively

Fear is an essential warning response to an unexpected situation. It is an appropriate emotional response in life-threatening situations such as walking near a precipice or facing an out-of-control car. In these situations the **amygdala** (part of the limbic system) is programmed to kick in with an automatic response commonly called **fight or flight**. In both of the above situations, flight would be the most appropriate response. We would recognise that through our perceptual interpretation of the events and environment around us.

Previous learning tells us what specific action to take, e.g. a careful retreat from the edge of the precipice or fast movement away from the car's path. A young child will often freeze in a similar situation because they have not learned what else to do, and this is the safest option in most cases.

Valuing all emotional messages

- ♦ To feel fear is not to be cowardly.
- ♦ To show fear is a sensible and honest response, part of self-preservation.
- ♦ To be ruled by fear is to be emotionally unable to function for our own best interests.

Fear is the basis of all limitations in our lives, however we rationalise it.

If presented with a challenge we might find our heart thumping, throat feeling dry, stomach churning and hands sweating. Whether we interpret that as fear would depend entirely on our perception. For instance, when facing an important exam, most students will feel all of the above physiological responses. What will differ will be their interpretation of these feelings as either (a) fear, or (b) excitement. The former will probably result in a retreat while the latter will engender a 'go for it' approach. Which student will succeed? Well, both might, but I suggest student (b) will do better and will certainly be more likely to want to repeat the experience, feeling that exams are a good challenge to rise to. Student (a) will probably avoid anything more than what is absolutely essential to 'get out of school free' and never sit another exam in their life.

> Experiences present us with choices. The emotional response we give is either our conscious or unconscious choice. The outcome is a result of the choice we make.

Try it now   Consider these points for a few moments in respect of your own life. If there is a choice of which subjective interpretation to use in relation to an experience, do you know how to make the better choice for yourself? Look back at your list of emotions for a day and see which list is longer, the joyful or the uncomfortable. How many emotional messengers are you keeping imprisoned? Make a note of any thoughts and feelings that come to you as you consider this and keep a record of them with your list. We will return to them again.

Recognising fear

The initial fear response kicks in whenever we face challenge or change, the unexpected. Yet as we saw in Chapter 1, change is the basis of realising potential and the single most important fact of life.

Variations on fear are:

- **anger** – fear of life not going as you had intended for yourself, of losing control
- **frustration** – fear of not getting what you want or perceive yourself to need
- **anxiety** – fear of failure, loss of face, fear of the future
- **cowardice** – fear of taking responsibility for own behaviours and emotions
- **sadness** – fear turned against ourselves, fear of loss or change
- **guilt** – fear of being wrong, of being accused of something or hurting someone
- **shame** – fear of getting 'found out', of being less than expected or demanded
- **regret** – fear of having lost something worth keeping
- **vengefulness** – fear of being 'a loser', of coming second, of not having the upper hand
- **bitterness** – fear of being cheated, of having less than you consider you deserve
- **jealousy** – fear of having or being less than someone else
- **hatred or dislike** – fear of that in another which reflects that behaviour/attitude in yourself
- **possessiveness** – fear of losing that which you have, fear of betrayal by others
- **self-pity** – fear of taking responsibility for own actions and experiences

- loneliness – fear of being unloved/unwanted, fear of being alone with self.

All these are based on a perception of the self as victim.

Experiencing joy

Joy is essentially the opposite of fear, and is energising and uplifting. It allows us to explore our potential in an emotional environment of confidence and expansion. If we experience a predominance of these emotions, we are likely to be contented and successful. We are not likely to avoid experiences and reduce our options in life. We are more likely to attract positive things into our life because we hold a positive emotional energy within us. We are likely to recognise our full potential and not feel afraid to develop it. We can also set the best possible example for all children.

Try it now   Think for a moment of the difference you feel being in the company of someone who is predominantly positive and cheerful, compared to someone who is predominantly negative and miserable. Which of these two would you prefer to be and which would you prefer your child to be? Which option would bring more chance of success in their life?

Recognising joy include:

Variations on joy
- **enthusiasm** – joy of opportunities being presented
- **elation** – joy of the experience in the present
- **calmness** – joy of general sense of well-being, spiritual contentment and health
- **peacefulness** – joy of sense of intimacy and fulfilment, joy of being alone with self
- **love** – joy of accepting others as they are and being accepted likewise
- **competence** – joy of developing skills and using them
- **confidence** – joy of exploring being yourself
- **self-esteem** – joy of knowing yourself and being true to that self

◆ **achievement** – joy of positive outcomes following sustained effort.

These two lists – variations of fear and variations of joy – are simplified explanations and will be discussed in greater detail in following chapters. The essential thing is to recognise which emotion you are experiencing and its origins. What is the message it wants you to hear?

Realising potential from the negative

For some people who have experienced a mostly fear-based life, it is still possible to achieve a degree of potential and certainly some types of success are bred from a basis of pain and fear, of anger and revenge. However, in the long run this will only work in certain areas of life and will often be a bitter success. The achievement is based on a perception of conflict and struggle. Who are we ultimately struggling with or in conflict with? Even if we are still in open conflict with a parent or another influence in our lives, we are ultimately in conflict with their power over us and our acceptance of their power to affect us. We are actually in conflict with ourself. Who will win, you or you?

When you fully recognise this you can also recognise how much energy is wasted in conflict and how much it is still a limited achievement. True achievement is only ever a positive experience with comfortable effort involved, and no losers. Any struggle implies inner conflict. Most of us have some.

Try it now

Look back at your chosen experiential day. Think about the experiences attached to the emotional response. Using the list of variations of fear, decide which forms of fear you were responding with. Now answer the following questions:

1 What purpose do these feelings have, what are they telling you about life's experiences?
2 What does this experience tell you about yourself?
3 What constructive action could you take to end any difficulty?
4 Are you wishing to impose your ideas of what should be on someone else?
5 Is there anyone you need to talk to in order to resolve this?

6   Are you really listening to the other people in this situation and empathising with their point of view?

7   What do you need to say or do to resolve the situation and achieve the outcome that is for the highest possible good for yourself *and* others?

8   Does your desire conflict with the highest possible good for yourself or others?

9   What else could you *choose* to think and feel?

10 Do you need/want to feel this emotion any longer?

Hopefully, this exercise will leave you more objective and conscious of your emotions and why you feel the way you do. Now try repeating the exercise with the positive feelings from your day. It is easy to take them for granted and overlook the ingredients. By exploring good feelings, we can re-create them using this recognition and understanding, thereby allowing us more choice in how we feel day to day.

Communicating successfully

Communication is the conveyance of thoughts, feelings and beliefs that underpin our perception of life. The language we use will indicate our perceptual basis as either fear or joy. Although we may think we are saying one thing, we are often saying something else. Understanding this enables us to consider what we really intend to communicate to our children.

Communication occurs on two levels. The first is the choice of actual words. This is a small part of the understanding, about 20 per cent. The second and bigger part of the communication is called the **meta-message** and is to do with all the assumptions, expectations, body language and contextual aspects of the communication. The meta-message is made up of the following:

- basis of interaction, intended outcome
- balance of power/authority
- emotional impact
- facial expressions and eye contact
- body posture and clothing worn
- environmental influences (context, venue, formal or informal)
- previous experiences with this person

- previous experiences in similar situations with others
- assumptions about intentions of other
- own intentions for interaction
- entire personal belief system about how life works
- entire social belief system about how life works and why.

Intuitively we learn to read all of these cues to reach the final understanding of a message, and although the choice of words is important, the rest is often where the difficulties lie.

Developing empathy

Empathy is central to effective emotional awareness in all areas of life.

> Empathy is the ability to imagine what it would feel like for you if you were in the same position as the person you are thinking of or talking to. How would you feel if someone were behaving towards you in the way that you are behaving towards them?

As a parent it is important to recognise and respect **how our children feel** so that we can respond to them sensitively and validate their experiences, taking them into account.

- We cannot relate to their feelings if we do not know our own.
- We cannot expect them to express their feelings to us if we do not teach them by example how to do this.

Try it now

Can you think back to a time when, as a child, you wanted to express yourself and no one took your seriously?

- How did this leave you feeling?
- Were you keen to communicate with this person again?
- Were you keen to communicate openly with anyone again?

The skills of empathy

Empathy has two main aspects to it:

1   the ability to imagine the situation from the other side, to put

yourself into someone else's shoes and to form relationships based on mutual appreciation and understanding

2   the skill of recognising that other people have a right to their point of view and taking this into account when you interact with them.

Try it now   Spend a few moments considering which of these you are good at and which you find more difficult. Think of examples when you have been able to do both and examples of when you have not. What was the difference?

Don't worry about how skilful you are at the moment, there is no competition here. It is simply important to recognise where you are right now so that you can develop these skills further. No one gets it right all the time but recognising where you make mistakes is the first step to improving your skills.

> Remember, making mistakes is an essential part of learning and improving in all areas of life, in realising one's full potential.

As parents it is essential to develop empathy skills and take into account your child's point of view for two reasons:

1   your child perceives that their experiences are considered significant and worthy of consideration, therefore they feel valued and worthy of consideration

2   your child recognises your skill in empathising with them and learns the same skill by following your example.

Try it now   A good exercise for refining empathy skills is to think back to a difficult situation. Briefly run through the incident in your mind, everything you felt, thought, said and did.

- What did you intend by those behaviours?
- How did the other party interpret them?
- What areas or aspects resulted in a difficulty?
- Was there a lack of two-way communication about what you really felt?
- Did you actually say what you really felt and wanted to say?

- Did you say things that only gave clues to what you wanted to say? What were they?
- Were you saying the opposite of what you wanted to say?
- Was the outcome as you had hoped for or intended?

There are no right or wrong answers. Your answers reflect your present position and should give you food for thought. The more you work with exercises like these, the better your understanding and self-knowledge will become. This process of self-development will enable you to teach your child the same skills and enhance your relationship with your child at the same time.

The second stage of this exercise is to imagine yourself as the other person in the same difficult situation or incident, trying to listen to you. Make sure that you are really in *their* position and not as you would like them to be, or as you think they should be.

- How easy was it for them to understand what you were saying?
- What level of frustration did they experience in being understood by you?
- What did they actually say in response to you?
- What was their understanding of your intended outcome?

Perhaps they felt equally frustrated in their attempts to get their point of view listened to. Perhaps they also failed to say exactly what they meant for fear of 'losing face' or being criticised for their experiences. Communicating with empathy means listening carefully as well as speaking carefully.

If you have difficulty being understood in relationships with parents, children, partners, etc., it is a reflection of how well you communicate and how easily they can understand you as well as how effectively you listen and take account of their position. All rows would begin and end as calm discussion if all communications worked. Fear blocks honest and successful communication, especially guilt and shame.

Case study: Keith and Jane

Keith and Jane are both divorcees who have set up home together. They each have one child. Jane lived alone for some time before meeting Keith and is not worried about being single again but would prefer to work with what they have. Keith walked straight out of his marriage and an affair, and latched onto Jane.

His biggest fear is to be alone. They have been together for three years and are finding it increasingly hard to agree on anything, even small decisions about the house. Jane suggests counselling. Keith says he would rather end the relationship than go to see a counsellor. Jane concedes. The relationship is easier for a while.

Two years later they are still arguing and Jane says she's had enough. She again suggests counselling or she feels that it is over for her. Keith agrees initially but then repeats that he would rather end the relationship than go for counselling. Jane agrees the relationship is over. Keith becomes very angry over the next few weeks and begins to bully Jane, shouting a lot and telling her that the relationship is over. She is not arguing with him. Then he starts throwing things round in the house and tells her that they can live together for another five years, until the children have grown up. Jane asks him to leave. He shouts even more loudly that their problem is that he just can't communicate with her any more. He is clearly very distressed. Jane does not feel able to communicate with Keith any more. _____

- ◆ What is happening between Jane and Keith and in their communications?
- ◆ Does Jane say what she means?
- ◆ Does Keith say what he means?
- ◆ Why can't Keith communicate with Jane?
- ◆ Why can't Jane communicate with Keith?

Perhaps Keith says what he thinks will get Jane to back down again. Is his anger a sign of his fear of being alone and frustration that his attempt to manipulate Jane is not working this time? Fear fills the relationship for Keith and he operates from this perception. Jane allowed herself to be bullied and manipulated before, which set up an expectation in Keith that this was how to keep the relationship together. His attempt to say what he really means comes through with such inner conflict that he expresses it aggressively. Jane cannot respond openly to what he has said because of the anger in his voice and the meta-message he is giving. He wants submission from Jane and he is increasingly fearful and shaken when it does not happen as he intends. She is fearful of his anger and desire to subjugate her and cannot say what she feels any more.

Clarifying communication outcomes

Whenever we are talking about something it is important to

understand where the discussion is left. Think back to your personal example of a difficult situation and your attempts at communication. Was the outcome of that discussion:

(a) a complete resolution and reconciliation?
(b) a compromise and avoidance of further dispute?
(c) another issue which remains unresolved and seething below the surface?

If you can answer yes to (a) then you are well on the way to successful communication skills. If you answered yes to (b) then you are possibly never dealing with anything and leave an undercurrent of difficulty that can build into resentment. If you answered yes to (c) then it would be a good idea to practise the above exercise as often as possible in all your interactions and notice the benefits to yourself and your life.

> All relationship crises are failures in communication and result from lack of empathy. This is true in professional, academic, personal and social relationships. Success is based on the ability to develop and use communication skills positively in all areas of our life.

Abusing empathy skills

Some people have excellent empathy skills but use them to manipulate others. This is called **playing games** and will be explored in greater depth in the next chapter. Utilising these skills in a negative way achieves a measure of success, which acts as a reinforcement to continue the behaviour. The success will always be short lived and cause more problems in the long run.

Defining success

Success comes in many shapes and forms. One of the most important rules is to avoid imposing your own set of values for measuring success on your child. If you let them devise their own, then they will work for it and stick to it with a motivation that would inspire you.

> A goal imposed from an external source, even from a beloved parent, is only achieved to please the parent, and therefore has limited intrinsic value to the child.

Try it now   Answer the following questions as quickly as you can. Give your immediate answer, not the answer that you would like to give. The more you consider these questions, the more likely you are to create the 'right' answer rather than explore your own deeper belief system and structures for success.

- What are your criteria for success?
- Which areas of life do you consider it important to be successful in?
- Do you consider yourself to be successful in all these areas?
- What were your parents' criteria for success?
- What do you perceive as society's criteria for success?

Referencing internally or externally

The more the child is freed from the pressure of external referencing for their own life, the better they will succeed in their life. The internally governed individual does not get drawn by other people, or become easily persuaded against their better nature. We will be referring to this theme several times during the book and in many different contexts.

One of the first researchers into potential and success was Abraham Maslow. He was a humanistic psychologist who looked at levels of achievement in the lives of many successful people like Einstein, Eleanor Roosevelt, Walt Whitman, Spinoza, Abraham Lincoln and Thomas Jefferson. He called success 'self-actualisation' – the realisation of all aspects of the potential of any individual, so that they reach the peak of their potential. Maslow also recognised that there is no such thing as the perfect human being.

Characteristics of self-actualisers

1 Perceive reality efficiently and accept uncertainty – 'go with the flow' approach to life.

2 Non-judgemental of self and others, accepting right for all to be as they are.

3 Spontaneity of thoughts and behaviours, able to work intuitively.

4 Problem-centred instead of self-centred, wanting to find solutions not to receive attention.

5 Unusual and non-judgemental sense of humour, often looking at life very unconventionally.

6 Able to look at life objectively, to step back and see what the truth is in any situation.

7 Highly creative and original in approaches to life, ready to challenge the 'norm'.

8 Retaining an independence but not purposely unconventional, retaining individuality.

9 Deeply appreciative of basic life experience, taking nothing for granted.

10 Establish deeply satisfying relationships with a few people.

12 Peak experiences, a sense of elation at their own experience of existence and achievement.

13 Embrace attitudes of equality for all, unimpressed by concepts of hierarchy and status.

14 Enjoy privacy and solitude, are comfortable with and not afraid to explore their own natures.

15 Hold strong moral or ethical standards to which they adhere in spite of external pressure.

Behaviours leading to self-actualisation

(a) Experiencing life with enthusiasm, absorption and concentration.

(b) Experimenting with new things and welcoming challenges instead of taking the 'safe path'.

(c) Listening to own feelings in evaluating experiences instead of accepting the assumptions of tradition, authority or the majority.

(d) Avoiding double-bind and game-playing behaviours; being honest.

(e) Being prepared to be unpopular when own perceptions do not coincide with peer groups.

(f)   Taking responsibility for own life and working hard for own goals.

(g)   Becoming fully aware of own emotions and being able to work with them consciously.

(h)   Identifying inappropriate defence mechanisms and having the courage to give them up through counselling or other means of self-help.

Try it now   Spend a few minutes considering the first of the above lists and think of experiences where you have, or have not, demonstrated each of the characteristics. How does each experience feel to you? What would you change if you could? What choices do you have?

Now consider the second list, behaviours, and see which of these describe you. Work as much as possible with feelings rather than intellectual thoughts. Thoughts can be manipulated to convey what we want to, but our feelings reflect our inner reality. Honesty with yourself is the best way to make progress in your own realisation of potential.

What is your assessment of yourself? Are you a self-actualiser or not? Do you inhibit or encourage self-actualising behaviours in your children? Were you encouraged to repeat self-actualising behaviours in your own childhood?

The story of Violet in Chapter 12 explains and demonstrates some of these points through two of the characters, Old Mags and Violet herself. In spite of her youth, Violet is a greater self-actualiser than either of her parents or most of the people in the village.

Exploring the importance of emotional competence

There are many ways in which emotional competence can be defined as important and it would be difficult to decide if one was more important than another. It is not always helpful to try and separate out specific areas as we are looking at achieving a life that is an overall success for our children and ourselves. A truly successful life is one where all aspects flow comfortably along with each other and are beneficial to others close to you, while any areas of difficulty are managed in a non-damaging way.

Ultimately, and in all areas of life, it is relationships that mark success or lack of it. This includes the relationship we have with ourself.

Maintaining relationships

If we do not know how to relate to ourselves, how can we relate to each other and build the relationships that fulfil our emotional needs and enrich our lives, either socially, at work or at home? Communication is the basis of all relationships and the effectiveness of communication decides the quality and cohesiveness of the relationship. The relationships we have with each other create small social groups, which collect to form the larger group we call **society**. Thus if we all improve our own relationship with ourselves, then with each other, we have the potential to build a better society. Maximising your own true potential does not limit others, it liberates them to do the same and to create a society which encourages individuality rather than conformity.

Social implications

Society is made up of individuals and we are all part of it. Society can be regarded as the sum total of what we are all saying, thinking, feeling and doing. Nothing happens without some sort of thought process. The governing influences of those thoughts are emotions and emotional experiences. Although logic can be a formative basis for thought, the final response always comes from emotional reactions. If we learn to create only positive thoughts and emotions, we begin to change society from within.

Individual and group perceptions

We cannot separate ourselves from society because it reflects us all. We cannot expect anyone to take responsibility for anyone else. We create our own reality through the subjective perceptual experience of society. For some it is full of potential and yet others perceive it as doom and gloom, with all the shades in between. It is the same society but the only difference is the perceptual viewpoint of the individual. One person's disaster is another's opportunity. Nothing else differs, only the perception and the history of emotions behind that interpretation. Thus Jane may see the ending of the relationship with Keith (see page 23) as a new beginning and recognise what she has learned from the relationship, or she may feel as if she is a victim deserted by yet another male. Her social group may prefer one or other of these two perceptions and seek to impose their view on her. Ultimately the choice is hers but the choice she makes will affect her whole future. It is an emotional choice.

Social or individual responsibility

There is an increasing recognition of social problems and debate over whose responsibility it is to sort it all out. We are all aware of rising violence in society and even children of five are demonstrating a capacity for considerable violence against each other. Clearly we are not talking about the normal rough and tumble of childhood, rather like the playful tangle of puppies or kittens that teaches them certain skills and tests their strength. Rather we are talking about the very real desire to inflict pain on other living beings.

This suggests a need to exert power over something or someone else. A need to do something, to behave in a certain way, is always a reflection of the inner emotions. So a need to have power over others is based on low self-esteem and self-awareness, a sense of powerlessness within the self. It is in direct contrast to self-acceptance, compassion and emotional competence. Children generally are not taught a compassionate approach to life, either directly or by example. There are exceptions to this in individual families who understand this principle, but in the main modern society does not understand it at all.

However, this is not the only crisis in our society. There are more relationship breakdowns, children taken into care, failures within the academic system, increased dependency on the state, dependency on chemicals, mental health problems, a growing phenomenon of incidental violence such as road rage and random mass killings. This is all to do with a lack of emotional intelligence and self-awareness in society and in individuals – a thwarting of the full potential that each and every one of us was born with.

No one can be held responsible for the behaviour of another human being. They can only be responsible for their response to the behaviour of other human beings. We each have to learn to be fully responsible for all our choices of behaviour.

We all need to develop emotional self-awareness in order to:

◆ develop and maintain close intimate relationships
◆ take responsibility for our own emotions and behaviour
◆ reduce stress in our lives, learning to respond rather than to react
◆ enable clear expressions of needs, thoughts and feelings
◆ improve mental and physical health
◆ enable learning to take place, both academic and social, without fear
◆ achieve our potential
◆ create a happier and more peaceful society.

None of us can take responsibility for others in achieving the above. As adults and parents we must do it for ourselves. Then we can begin to rear a generation of children who have the emotional competence to create that better society.

Learning together

The most important point to make here is that **we are all doing the best with what we know.** There is no exception to this rule. Even someone who clearly knows what they are doing and is conscious of their bad behaviour, even they are doing their best because they have yet to learn that there are better ways of getting the results they seek without resorting to violence, bullying, unkindness, etc. Consider the story of The Fox and the Blue Grapes. Think of Violet's father (See Chapter 12). It is often not until later that we realise our mistakes and see that we could have made other choices. But for some, admitting they might be wrong is not an option. These people are unable to see that they repeatedly re-create their own difficulties. And they keep behaving in the only way they know how. The kind of stress produced by such inner conflict has long been associated with self-pity and depression. Putting increased effort into the behaviour does not make it suddenly become an effective response either, it only makes the outcome more extreme.

> If we keep doing what we have always done, we will keep getting the same outcomes. To change the outcomes for ourselves we must first change our own behaviour patterns.

Avoiding learning

The biggest barrier to learning is fear of change. However much we complain about things, most people do not want to change. They want someone else to do so instead. They want their position to remain as it is and life to change around them. This is a desire to control life. And we don't really want others to change in a way that we cannot control any more either. We feel threatened by changes in people close to us, so we continue to complain and do not really want anyone or anything to change at all.

Yet the courage to make those changes can result in a very different life. Getting it wrong first enables us to appreciate how good it really can be when you are open to the learning process. So getting it wrong is not a problem as long as we recognise what it is that we are doing and change accordingly. Two emotions, regularly taught as a means of control, prevent this more than anything else:

◆ guilt
◆ shame.

These are discussed in greater detail in the next chapter.

Parenting, a new learning opportunity

Having children represents a need for continuous change. From confirmation of the pregnancy onwards, parents have options:

◆ They can resist change and make the experience as difficult for each other and their child as possible.
◆ They can predict change and try to control the process, maintain the status quo, force things to go along the path they think they should.

- They can be open to the new experiences and learn new emotional responses as they arise, allowing life to lead them joyfully to self-realisation and manifestation of full potential.

Children provide many opportunities for you to learn and change.

Understanding mirroring

If we recognise that children can teach us much about ourselves, we can learn from them and teach them what we have learned. They act as **mirrors**. If there is something they do which you find uncomfortable, it is likely to be a reflection of you. With young children especially, where else has that behaviour come from? Learn from their simple demonstration of you and accept the opportunity. If you feel angry, take time to reflect and see if you can discover the root cause of that response. You do not have to like your children but if you don't, you probably don't like yourself and they probably won't like you either. Are they too similar for comfort? Only you can change that.

Summary

Parenting can be a rewarding and enriching experience that extends and challenges us if we allow it. In order to be emotionally aware and balanced in our approach to all aspects of our life, it is important to recognise what emotions are and how we can use them for our own best interests.

- Learn to identify emotions and their root causes, the message they are conveying.
- Recognise that we can choose how to respond to all experiences.
- Learn how to use empathy for the good of the other and yourself.
- Define success and recognise blocks to learning and developing.
- Identify opportunities for learning and accept change as always positive and inevitable.
- Identify the significance, for the individual and for society, of emotional competence.
- Accept that we are *all* doing our best with what we know.
- Understand and value mirroring from your child, recognising your own need for learning.

CHAPTER 3

Exploring Emotional Choices

E ach and every aspect of life, every day, consists of making choices. These choices include how to feel, think and behave both in the immediate present and in relation to both the past and the future. Most of the time we as adults are not even considering life as a process of decisions. We are effectively on automatic pilot and going through the daily ropes as if we are asleep in our own lives.

Children are born with an awareness of everything, endlessly fascinated by why and how and where. They get the most out of each and every day – and slowly they are taught to lose this wonderful sense of magic. Most adults perceive this as 'growing up'. But if we stop and consider the following questions, we might begin also to question our own perceptions.

- Is it really necessary to lose the sense of full awareness of, and absorption with, every activity as it occurs, and every aspect of life, in order to grow up?
- Is this what growing up should require of us, or are there other reasons why we lose the sense of adventure in life?
- How much are we missing and how can we change this to make the most of each and every day?
- How can we make each day into a day well lived, ending with a feeling of satisfaction, without feeling stressed out and depleted?
- As success in life depends on making the best choices, how can we teach our children to do this when we ourselves do not?

As role models for our children, it is important that we become more aware of the choices we all have in life and become fully conscious of all the choices we make. This has several advantages for us as parents:

1 We can make better choices in our roles as parents and in the way we manage our children, whatever age they are now.

2 The more we make conscious choices for ourselves, the more we can show our children how to do this for themselves.

3 We actually begin to improve the quality of our own lives at the same time.

Making choices

We make different kinds of choices in all our activities:

- unconscious choices that come out as automatic responses
- habits that are choices we no longer give any consideration to
- conscious choices and difficult decisions made as a result of in-depth thought
- routines that we have chosen, developed and use for efficiency, no longer considering their value
- emotional reactions to some news from a media source or friend, or to our children's needs and behaviour
- changes in a routine or habit for a day, choosing to do something differently
- taking a new look at something and changing our opinion
- maintaining the opinion we have always held in our lives
- accepting the way life develops itself for and around us
- feeling as if we are a victim of the difficult circumstances of our lives.

Avoiding the automatic

All of these are choices and there are many, many more. Unconscious and automatic choices are useful for efficiency and the human brain is designed to create these routines or patterns. The mistake is to allow our whole lives to become automatic. It is almost as if we are no longer aware of what we are feeling or doing in our lives. We are on automatic pilot because we have found it too hard, too challenging, to wake up to what we are really doing and saying, thinking and feeling.

> Even the decision we make not to think about what we are doing, each and every day, is a choice we have made. So we cannot avoid the responsibility for all areas of our lives.

Try it now   Start this activity as early in the day as possible. Make a list of all the choices you have made so far today. This should include the choice to get out of bed, of what to wear, what to eat, what to say to people. Remember, every single activity is the result of a choice at some level. Activities done automatically are still choices, but they are ones that we have not considered, we have just carried them out. Are there any decisions that you have already made to day, that you would change and do differently?

This activity will help you to recognise just how important the skill of making choices or decisions can be.

- A skilful choice becomes effortless success in all aspects of life, allowing us to realise our potential.
- An unskilful choice becomes a source of difficulty if we let it, a limitation and drain on our energies and resources.
- If we remain open to learning from everything in life and accept the need for change, an unskilful choice can become a source of learning and therefore equally valuable.

Being in control

One of the biggest mistakes we make is to believe that we are not in control of our minds, our thoughts and our feelings, our behaviour and physical body. We say things like:

- 'I couldn't help it.'
- 'It's not my fault.'
- 'If that hadn't happened I would have done this instead.'
- 'It's because of this happening in my childhood.'
- 'Other people do it so why shouldn't I.'
- 'I will behave like that when others do it too. I'm not going to be the only one.'

Mostly we tend to blame others or circumstances or the past for the choices that we made right here and now. All the above statements avoid responsibility for our own behaviour. Yet our body, our mind and our feelings are only aspects of us. So who is in control of us? The reason we may not be in control is because we are not aware of what is actually happening to us in life and what we are truly capable of. To make a study of self-awareness is generally thought to be a form of vanity, weakness or selfishness. We teach people to look outside of themselves all the time and then wonder why we do not know what is going on inside. So we are missing all the information we need in order to make better choices in life. And this is the key to leading a contented and successful life.

> If emotions are the messengers of experience and we do not recognise them, we are missing the richness of most of the experiences of our own lives.

In order to learn from experience and move on, to avoid painful repetitions for our own sakes, we have to be prepared to explore our past experiences and recognise what it is we need to change within us.

Breaking the power of shame and guilt

Our lack of conscious awareness in life is a form of protection against the responsibility of making so many choices – or rather, avoiding the **shame** and **guilt** that comes with making 'mistakes', as they are viewed in our culture.

In the main we can accept that fear is the basis of all the negative emotions and all the difficult experiences. However, there are two primary emotional states: joy and fear (see Chapter 2). Joy is our natural state, so any sense of fear at any level causes us to be separated from our true sense of self, our true state of joy. Everything we feel that is negative is a sign of our separation from our whole sense of self.

Guilt and shame are actually quite similar to each other, although they can be stimulated by widely differing experiences. They come from a single sense: a fear that we are not good enough and it is only a matter of time before everyone else realises how inadequate we are. The more guilt and shame we feel, the more inadequate we believe ourselves to be.

Examining the truth about guilt

Superficially, guilt is a fear of:

+ being found out that you are less than perfect
+ being less than you would like to be seen as
+ being things that you don't want other people to know about.

However, it is actually more about your perception of yourself as being less than you would like yourself to be. Or being unable to make the choices that you would want to make. It comes from a feeling of 'being wrong to be as you are'. It is a lack of self-acceptance, a lack of acceptance of your human fallibility, that you are going to make mistakes from time to time.

Recognising cultural attitudes

There are far too many examples of a social perception that any mistakes you make are merely confirmation of how inadequate you really are. In the main our society takes the attitude that mistakes must be punished rather than viewed as an opportunity for learning. The bigger the mistake, the more guilt and shame is heaped upon us, and the more we are made to feel that we are a 'bad person'. Feeling guilty becomes our sense of normal. And if we feel that we are a bad person we will usually behave in this way until we recognise that we have different choices to make for ourselves and that we are worth making those choices for.

Building healthy self-esteem in everybody is the key to a successful and contented life for all and a crime-free society.

So we are taught to feel guilty for being all that we can be and for doing our best, however unskilful that is. But if we feel guilty about being who we are, does this bring out the best behaviour in us? Does this enable us to accept our mistakes and learn from them?

Internal and external perspectives

Shame is the fear of other people seeing that you are not the person that you would really like to be. Both shame and guilt can be used by ourself against ourself, or by others against us if we let them. Other people can make us feel guilty, or we can feel ashamed of ourselves without anybody else being involved.

The difficulty is that both shame and guilt are based on the idea that:

♦ who we really are isn't a very nice/right/good person, we are wrong to be as we are
♦ who we want to be is the nice person that we pretend to be and that isn't the truth
♦ someone might find out 'the truth' about us and blow the whistle, reject us.

So there is a denial of our whole self and this creates the sense of separation from the true self, which is both; all the good and all the mistakes too. We are human, full of great things and some not very skilful things.

Understanding illusions

Like all fears, guilt and shame are based on an illusion that we are taught and then continue to re-create for ourself. And because we re-create it, we believe it and because we believe it, it becomes a reality. But illusions are like shadows. When you turn the light on them, they disappear. The shadow might appear somewhere else, or appear in a different form, but if you put enough lights on you don't get any shadows. So it is like turning the lights on into the shadows, saying 'do I need this'?

Try it now Think of something that you have said or done at some point in your life that makes you feel guilty or ashamed. Spend some time thinking what this experience has taught you and answer these questions:

1 How could you do this differently next time?
2 Did you do your best at the time with what you knew?
3 If you had known more would you have done things differently?
4 How would you approach this situation now?
5 Are you ready to forgive yourself for the mistake you have made and to learn from it?

6   Are you ready to accept responsibility for your own behaviour and action, your own choices?

7   Are you open to the wonderful opportunity these experiences offer, to learn how to do things differently next time?

8   Do you still need to feel guilty or ashamed? And did you ever need to?

9   How do you feel right now and what could you do that demonstrates your new understanding?

This exercise should help you to recognise that you do not need to carry any guilt or shame around, and therefore you are less likely to pass it on to your child.

Healing our feelings

When we turn the spotlight on feelings of guilt and shame and recognise them for what they really are, which is an illusion, we can then start to eradicate them. As parents we can help to heal our own feelings like this and we can also make sure we do not re-create them in our own children.

Case study: Keith _____

Keith has difficulty saying what he feels. His father was rarely approachable and as a child, Keith was scared of him. No matter how hard Keith tried to please his father, he felt a failure because he did not win approval but was encouraged to continue working for it. And whatever he did, fault was found with it. He was rarely allowed to feel good about anything he had achieved throughout childhood and felt deeply ashamed of any flaws in everything he did. Perfection became the unattainable goal. It was a 'no win' situation for Keith. _____

Perpetuating self-judgement

As an adult, Keith is always highly critical of himself and others. Inside he is ashamed of all that he does, waiting for the moment of discovery by others, the public revelation of his inadequacy. He behaves in ways that increase his feelings of guilt and shame because this is what he knows and feels used to. At the same time he is always looking for ways to get away from these feelings, and giving them to other people seems to work. His life focus is avoiding responsibility and dwelling in a fear of the past, of what he will be found out for, and a fear of the future, of what or who will finally uncover the truth.

Thinking into the past and future

There is absolutely no need to feel either guilt or shame in our lives. They serve no useful purpose and are based on either the past or the future. They are never based on the immediate now.

> Guilt and shame occur simply because we are not thinking 'Right here, right now, we are all doing the best we can with whatever we each know.'

We are thinking that in the next half-hour, or in the next week, or in the next month something will happen that will show us up, catch us out. So we are projecting either forwards or backwards and that is where the difficulty is coming from. We are hanging on to old beliefs and hurts or we are creating potential hurts and struggles that haven't even happened yet. What we are not doing is focusing on 'Right here, right now, I am doing all that I can do, I am doing my best. Everything is fine.'

Seeing the real story

All the evidence suggests that if we learn to trust and let go of those fears then all our fears will dissolve and we can actually experience the full potential of life. This is what it means to fully realise the potential of any individual in their life. And if this is what we want to teach our children so that they can lead more successful lives, then we must start right here with ourselves. We must also learn to live freely and be open to the learning in all that life brings us. Everything starts from within. It is our lack of trust in ourselves that causes us to believe we are inadequate and to have feelings of guilt and shame. It is also this lack of trust that maintains the idea that we will always get it wrong, that we will be wrong next week, we are wrong now and that we were wrong in the past.

Being wrong

One of the difficulties is: what is wrong? What is right and what is wrong? Who has the monopoly on being right?

Being right or wrong is different for different people. What we want and what we need in life might not be the same thing. So we might think we have got something wrong but in fact it was exactly right for us at that point in life. It taught us what we needed to know if we bothered to look and recognise the lesson. This is why being fully aware is so important to all aspects of life. All mistakes come from not being fully aware of all our choices and not seeing the real story. What we really need most is to learn the next lesson in life so that we can become more skilful. Then we can move on and make a better choice next time.

Case study: the effects of guilt and shame on Keith's adult life _____

As an adult Keith often moves from job to job and tries to work alone. He often misses opportunities for promotion and developing his potential yet achieved overall grade A's at school. He has never maintained a steady relationship. He has regular affairs alongside any longer relationships, including a marriage with a daughter. Although he is desperate to settle down and feel secure, he flirts with anyone who responds because he has learned how to charm and win superficial approval.

For Keith love is a battle of wills, of seeking and gaining approval, of fighting for control and dominance. He cannot respond to requests or suggestions from his partner because he hears it only as yet another rejection of all the effort he is making. He 'tests' his partners to see how much they love him, and tries to force Jane into loving him unconditionally, no matter how badly he treats her (see page 23). He threatens to end the relationship in order to make Jane 'try harder' for him but feels fear when she begins to withdraw from him. Keith is left feeling hurt and confused about why all the women in his life treat him like this. He just needs to find 'the right partner' and he keeps on looking, flirting and desperately seeking approval from wherever he can. _____

- ◆ Which dominant emotion does Keith live with?
- ◆ What is the long-term future likely to be for Keith?
- ◆ What is the real cause of Keith's emotional and relationship failures?

The fear of failure and rejection kicks in for Keith as soon as he starts to become close to someone and blocks all real communication. He uses his own understanding of feeling hurt as a basis for attacking his partners with the intention of undermining their confidence and sense of security. By making them feel or appear less confident and relaxed, he feels more confident by contrast. This is a perceptual difference. Keith feels fear and assumes the source of his fear is his partner, i.e. external. He does not realise that it is a fear programme in him and has little to do with his partner. He reacts to his fear and the loving partner becomes undifferentiated from the hostile attacker, so he counter-attacks. He uses empathy to hurt and to wield power, as his father did over him.

Keith is very like the fox in the story of The Fox and the Blue Grapes in Chapter 11. He lives from an emotional basis of fear – fear of losing what he has got. But his fear-based behaviours create exactly what he most dreads happening, destroying loving relationships and driving people away. Thus his belief in not trusting people is continually reinforced. Childhood is the learning ground for this approach.

Damaging communication styles

There is a particular style of communication which leads to these difficulties, called the **double bind**. First introduced as a theory by Bateson in the 1950s, it has become a basis for much work in the areas of family therapy. It denotes a system where the communication purports to be about one thing but there is a deeper and more significant, unspoken message occurring at the same time. No one actually says exactly what they mean but they give clues and attempt to manipulate other members of the familiy into doing, thinking or saying what they want. Then they can deny responsibility for the outcome because they didn't actually say it. Parents use it with their children in many ways. It puts the recipient in a 'no win' situation, where their own feelings are totally discounted and they have to find a way to demonstrate their love for the parent in order to keep their approval.

Identifying needs

Your needs may not be to have an easy comfortable life, may not be to have millions of pounds coming your way. More importantly, your needs are **not to get it right all the time.** Your need may be to learn that challenges can reveal the strength in you – and to teach your children, by example, how to make better choices in their lives.

That may be your need, but we often perceive it as a difficulty, as something that we don't want to have to deal with. Our perception is that there is something bad happening here. That is the difficulty, because it is the belief in two powers, in good and bad, right and wrong. So we need to think about whether this is actually a bad experience or not, or if this is a situation that we can actually learn something from.

Choosing ways of interpreting experience

If we are faced with a situation that makes us feel insecure and uncertain and brings out our feelings of guilt and shame, then what we are being shown is that we don't need those feelings. But we do still have them inside us and that is why we need to get rid of them. As with all these things, it is as difficult as we make it. What we all need to realise is that these are ideals, we will all get there eventually, there is no rush and we have to be compassionate with who we are now. These same principles should apply to the way we deal with our children.

The point is, when we realise where we could be heading, it makes it easier to move from where we are now, but it doesn't mean that we are going to get from here to there in one go. So the more you pull yourself out of these negative beliefs that you hold, the better your ability to make wise choices.

Recognising the biggest choice

All aspects of fear result in us blocking the full realisation of our potential. If we are caught up in these negative emotions, they prevent us from expressing who we really are, with all the love and compassion that we actually have. All of us are potentially loving, compassionate people. It's just that things make us go 'Urgh, I am not going to love there' or 'I'm not going to feel compassionate there' and we close ourselves off because we feel we need to protect ourselves.

But actually, underneath it all, wouldn't you say that we all desire to be loving and compassionate to everybody and for everybody to have the same response to us? It is a lovely goal to go towards. If people say it is completely unrealistic to think that we can ever get there, that is their cynicism and fear that they cannot achieve that goal. I prefer to believe that it's unrealistic to think that we won't get there. Anyway, what is wrong with aspiring?

Acceptance is part of potential

We are denying ourselves access to our own *whole* love of *self*, in other words, a total self-acceptance. It is an acceptance of all the things that may have questionable aspects to them. It is an acceptance that perhaps we all have qualities that have to be dealt with in different ways. It is moving away from these fears:

- that we are less than adequate
- that we cannot meet our own needs.

The truth is that you have actually coped with everything life has sent, so you have always met your own needs, you have always survived. It might have felt like you weren't going to, but actually you always have, haven't you? Otherwise you wouldn't be here right now.

Ask yourself these questions:

- Who is meeting your needs?
- Who has always met your needs?
- Who understands and recognises your needs?
- Who lives inside your emotions and thoughts?
- Who will always be able to meet your needs?

Who else, indeed, but you?

Taking responsibility

Once we are able to recognise that we are the only person who can meet our own needs, and start to take responsibility for that for ourself, we can begin to find out all that we are capable of. As long as we depend on someone else to meet our needs, we are open to betrayal, disappointment and failure because we are asking someone else to put us first but we are not prepared to do it for ourself.

So ultimately we have two choices:

1   If we, as parents, can really start to put this into practice in all aspects of our own lives, we can also begin to teach our children to do the same.

2   But if we continue to make choices to act unconsciously and to give others the responsibility for our life, we will teach our children this model of living.

One is based on realising all of your own potential, the other is based on limitation and fear.

Do you completely trust that whatever situation comes up you will be able to survive it and cope with it and deal with it and move on from it? Or do you feel, 'I don't want this to happen, I won't be able to cope with that. Help, help, help . . . .' We are scared of being inadequate. Yet the truth is that we are more than adequate to cope with all that life can throw at us, because we have always coped until now. But we *believe* that we haven't because we believe that somehow we should have done things differently, better. Somehow it shouldn't have happened. These are the illusory beliefs that teach us to fear what might happen next.

One of these illusory beliefs is that we should be ashamed or feel guilty for what has happened in the past. Consequently, we become fearful and as a result limitation sets in.

Case study: Megan and Keith

Megan and her father Keith have been living with Jane and Sam for five years now. Megan is close friends with both Jane and Sam. But Keith and Jane separate after many rows. Megan wants to stay friends. Jane says she would like that too but that Megan must tell Keith. Her father then highlights the perceived injustices that Jane and Sam have apparently heaped on him and ridicules them. The next time Megan sees them, she is hostile and tells Jane she doesn't want to see her and Sam any more. Jane says she understands and if Megan changes her mind she will be happy to see her.

This is not an uncommon story. It happens all the time in all sorts of contexts as parents have problems with their relationships. It is just as likely to happen with birth parents. But it is always possible to learn from mistakes.

♦   What are the choices that Megan has been given in this situation?

- How has empathy been used?
- Why is this an example of the double bind?
- Was it really Megan's choice not to see Jane and Sam any more?
- Who listened to Megan's wishes?
- Whose needs were considered before hers?
- What is the meta-message to Megan?
- What emotions has Megan experienced with this episode in her life?
- What is the basis behind Keith's behaviour?

Megan probably experienced most of the following: separation and loss of friendship, guilt, being wrong, frustration, regret, sadness and fear of similar rejection from her father. Her father can point out that it is Megan's choice because he hasn't actually said 'don't see Jane and Sam'. Megan has been made to feel sorry for him instead, and to prioritise his feelings in order to prove her love for him. Keith feels too insecure to allow Megan to continue as friends with Jane and Sam **because if she still likes them they cannot be as bad as all that, can they?** So he loses his justification for rejecting them. He cannot accept that he has failed another relationship. Keith's behaviour may finally bring rewards and an appearance of success in achieving his intended outcomes, but is this success and is it what he wanted?

Keith could have ensured Megan's love for him in many other ways, but he has not learned to trust other people. He believes that he has to manipulate her in order to protect himself and her love for him, as his father taught him and treated him. He was doing the best he could for himself with what he knew, and in many ways he intended the best for Megan too, from his point of view. Since he could not trust anyone, neither should she. He was teaching her the only self-protection he knew. Every time it failed him, as with the breakdown of so many relationships and job changes, this was evidence for him of how right he was not to allow himself to trust anyone and openly say what he feels and thinks.

Recognising the potential to change

One important thing to remember in life is the reality of continuous and absolute change. The person you are today is not the same as the person you were yesterday. There are aspects that are the same, there is a continuity in your consciousness, your thoughts and feelings, but you are not the same person. Even in the last ten minutes you have read things that may have changed you. Realising potential means accepting that this process of continuous and perpetual change is desirable, that nothing is permanent, including ourself. We retain qualities that give a *sense* of permanence but we are not permanent. Nothing is. We want permanence because we believe that it is something to be desired, but there is no permanence.

Understanding the nature of change

In order to fully appreciate the nature of change, I want to use the example of an apple. When does the apple begin and when does the apple end? It never began and it never ends. It always exists but it doesn't always exist as an apple. At some point it was a very small apple but before that it was a flower and before that a bud, a twig, an apple seed that grew into the tree that produced the apple. After it has become the apple it will fall on the ground and either be eaten and become part of someone's body and pass through them into the ground, or rot away and sink into the ground and the seed grow into a new apple tree.

Where did the apple begin and end? It never begins and it never ends, it just changes. And we are like that apple, we are always growing and changing. We go through the seasons of our life. Each year we celebrate our birthdays and each year we change. Every day of our lives we change.

Becoming compassionate to self

If we can allow ourselves to make mistakes and learn from the lessons, to go with the flow, we no longer need to feel ashamed of who we were and what we have done, because that person no longer exists. And right here, right now, maybe we wouldn't make the same mistakes. To judge ourself on something we did in the past is incredibly unkind. We have no reason to feel guilty and we have no reason to feel ashamed of who we were. What we must always remember, when struggling with these emotions, is to be compassionate with ourselves as parents and also with our children. It is really about choosing how we respond from now on, realising that it is up to us how we deal with these things.

- We can choose to be harsh on ourselves or we can choose compassion.
- We can choose to carry on as we have always done or we can make changes.
- We can experiment with changes and allow ourself to learn from each new approach.

Being wrong is good for us

There is one rule about the way we change or do things: it doesn't matter whether we get it wrong or right, just the fact that we are prepared to try it in a different way means that we are starting to move. We might get it wrong again and again but we are learning about getting it wrong, so when we know what getting it wrong means, then we can start to really get it right and we never have to go back to ever getting it wrong again.

Valuing the mistakes we have made is very important because that is part of the learning. But it does take a great deal of discipline to change. We have to make a conscious choice not to do this any more. If we find we are still doing it because it is an old habit, an old pattern we are stuck with, we have to say, 'Oops, slap on the wrist, we *are* going to change.' We have made the commitment not to do it that way and keep a gentle, compassionate pressure on ourselves to do things in a new way.

Summary

Realising your potential and making a success in all areas depends on several approaches to life:

- recognising and becoming conscious in all our choices in life
- accepting the need for change and experimentation
- accepting that mistakes are an essential part of learning
- releasing limiting beliefs and emotions, especially guilt and shame
- recognising the positive in everything, no matter how much we struggle with it
- taking full responsibility for all aspects of our own life and our own choices.

CHAPTER 4

Skilful Parenting

S o far we have looked at common human experiences and applied them to parenting in a general way. It is time now to begin looking specifically at the task of parenting. The more skilful we are in our own emotional lives, the more skilful we will be as parents.

> Parenting should be a case of 'do what I say **and** what I do'.

It is important to remember that there is no single correct way to be a parent. We can make better or less skilful choices in our role as a parent. Compassion is probably more significant here than in any other part of your life – in particular, compassion for yourself and the lessons you will have to learn. The more self-acceptance you can develop for yourself as a parent, doing your best and learning as you go, the better role model you provide.

Evolving parenting skills

We are not born with parenting skills and they do not come with puberty or in a neat package of instructions on arrival of the first child. They reflect our emotions and communication skills in the present and our need to evolve as the child develops and changes.

Parenting skills reflect our own self-awareness, of how we think, feel and behave towards ourselves and our children. Parents with more than one child will probably recognise that they use different skills with different children, in accordance with:

- age
- gender
- relationship styles
- personality
- interactions within the family

- other factors within the extended family
- social/environmental factors
- resources, both material and emotional.

There is no easy stage in parenting. Every stage presents challenges and opportunities for learning. As parents we evolve with our children.

Parenting beliefs

Before the child is born parents have experiences and assumptions that form a theoretical starting point for the work ahead. This is our perceptual belief system of what being a parent means and consists of a complex mixture of acceptance and rejection of ideas from the following sources:

- own childhood experiences
- observation of sibling childhood experiences
- own parents' styles and approaches
- parents' relationships with grandparents
- advice from books and experts
- observation of others around you
- media influences and attitudes
- extended family value systems
- peer groups.

Learning from the past

Most of the difficulties we have in our adult life come from the childhood struggles that we have not yet positively utilised and learned from. A buried conflict is never a resolved conflict. Having your own children is more than likely to bring old issues right back to the surface. It is very important here to remind yourself to be compassionate with your own parents too. They did the best they could with what they knew, however unskilful that was at the time.

Accepting an opportunity to change

Through our new role as a parent, we have the opportunity to revisit our own childhood experiences, gaining perspectives that differ from the view held as a child. Many new parents turn to

their own mothers and fathers and say that they now understand
the difficulties their parents faced. This is a time for healing old
arguments and developing new relationships as adults and equals,
with experiences of parenting in common.

Recognising good and bad lessons

We have all learned parenting skills from our own parents. This
can take two forms:

1 We can recognise things we appreciate from our childhood and
   pass examples of good practice on to our children. This is an
   opportunity to appreciate our positive experiences.
2 We can recognise difficult areas and use this as 'a lesson in how
   not to do it'. This means taking a negative experience from our
   past and making it positive for the present and the future.

Our own childhood is a valuable resource for developing skilful
parenting choices. Above all, it is important to recognise that,
whether our own childhood felt predominantly easy or a struggle,
it was the making of us as we are now.

> We can never change the past but we can use those valuable
> lessons to their fullest advantage with our own children.

Perpetuating damaging parenting experiences

Too often adults who had difficult experiences in childhood are
too angry with their own parents to see the learning potential, the
real value of those experiences. That anger will affect our children
and result in perpetuating our experiences through our parenting
styles. Keith is passing his fear on to Megan, his daughter (see
page 46). He lives with an image of a frightened, rejected little boy
inside and is responding with that child's emotions. His inner
child is damaged and without healing himself, the damage is
perpetuated.

Most of us carry around inside the wounded child that we were.
The work of healing consists of:

1 **Acceptance.** Accepting that you cannot change other people,
   you cannot change the past and you cannot make things

different. Acceptance is just letting things be as they are, knowing that we cannot change them, and not letting them affect you any more.

2 **Forgiveness.** Recognising that people who feel good about themselves do not hurt other people. So if our parents caused us any hurt, it was a reflection of their own lack of self-awareness and self-acceptance. The pain they inflicted on us was mirroring of the pain they felt inside. We can forgive their human frailty as we forgive our own.

3 **Compassion.** Any parent would want to do their best for their child as much as they can, including many parents who are called abusive. The problem is that they do not know how to because they have too much hurt inside them. So we can feel compassion for the level of hurt still inside our parents and ourselves and resolve to end it now.

Once you begin to work with these processes for yourself, you will probably find that all your relationships improve.

Healing the inner child

Antenatal lessons should be less about how to feed the baby and more about how to heal your inner child and release negative experiences so that your own birth-child can benefit from your lessons. You will benefit by releasing old negative emotions and re-creating a positive childhood experience. This should be done regularly because as your child grows, unresolved issues from different stages through your own childhood will resurface.

Try it now

The best way to identify old and buried wounds is to think about what creates a strong emotional response, good or bad. Use your notes from the first exercise in Chapter 2 (page 13) to identify those strong emotions and their source. Once you have identified where your strongest emotional responses are located, you can begin to examine them for what they are telling you. Remember the idea of mirroring: that all experience in life is a mirror of what we feel inside at some level or another.

- Is your joy based in acceptance, feeling safe, in control, confident, having things, enjoying activities?

- Is your difficulty with self-esteem, feeling insecure, wanting material security, wanting things to be as you like them?

The next stage of this exercise requires that you really examine your difficult experiences.

- Write a list of your principal areas of difficulty, then choose one to work on. You can work through the rest later.
- Look at what that difficult experience taught you. This is what **you had to be** to cope with the decisions that your parents made. Are you, for instance, determined, assertive, gentle, kind, independent? Did you work hard at school to prove them wrong? Did you become passive, quiet, easily content? Look for positive outcomes, wherever they are.

All experiences develop active and passive behaviours as survival skills. Active responses are confrontational, rejecting, fighting skills and the ability to make better choices. Passive responses are the areas where we yielded, learned compromise, and developed peace-keeping skills. All have their value and everyone has a different balance. The important thing to remember in life is not what happens but how you perceive it, then and now. It is always possible to find a positive outcome in everything.

- How do those skills and qualities benefit you now?
- Is there any other way that your parents could have taught this?
- What would your life be like now if you had not developed this ability or quality?
- Are you still angry with your parents, or life, and does it help to be?

You may have to practise this exercise many times. Keep reminding yourself of what you know until it fully permeates your emotions. When you no longer feel any emotional response to the original stimuli, you know you are healed.

Loving the inner child

Another way of approaching the issues of self-acceptance, forgiveness and compassion is to work with an actual image of yourself that you can relate to in some way. We all carry a mental image of ourself as a child. So is yours loved and cherished or rejected and denied by you?

Try it now   Find a photograph of yourself as a young child and look yourself in the eye. Recognise all the courage and strength, all the ingenuity that this child needed in order to get to where you are now. Tell that child how much you empathise with all their difficulties and how well they've done with what they knew. Send that child messages of love, daily.

Recognising your own resistance

Quite probably as you work through these exercises you will find a reluctance to adopting these new perspectives because it means that all those problems which caused you so much grief were actually good for you. This does not mean that the experiences were good, or that we were 'wrong' or 'bad' children and deserved them. But we do not want to let the 'offender get away with it' and forgiveness is often mistakenly assumed to be the same as agreement. It is never this. Forgiveness is only ever for our own benefit, and never for the other person/people involved, whoever they are. We might think we are making them pay as they watch us continue to hurt ourself, through our own anger and fear. But it is no longer their actions hurting us. It is only our own.

The past continues to hurt only if we let it. Releasing negative childhood experiences is central to developing the successful parenting skills that allow you to nurture your own child's potential. Children are like sponges, they absorb our emotional energies and adopt our emotional patterns. An angry or frightened parent will produce an angry or frightened child.

> If we remain angry and hurt by our own childhood experiences, we pass that on to our children.

Exploring power relationships in parenting

All relationships have a power element, based on who makes the decisions and sets the agenda, whose values are the dominant ones and who takes responsibility. With a young baby the parents have total power. Balance is established by parents giving the child a degree of empowerment. A good example of this is how parents respond to a crying child:

- ◆ If they always rush to give attention to a crying child, they are giving the child the power to summon mum or dad whenever they wish. The child has too much power.
- ◆ If they never respond quickly at all, then they are clearly in total control and leaving the child feeling very helpless and powerless.
- ◆ If they respond to the child without appearing to rush to meet their every whim, they demonstrate to the infant that their needs are recognised and their expressions of distress and need for attention are respected, but not above all else. A balance of power for all.

Power and authority

The balance of power continues to vary and develop throughout your relationship. Children will challenge the power of parents as figures of authority all the way. Although this can be very annoying, it is essential as part of their own developing sense of how to manage life. Power and authority are issues for all of us. How much we defer to authority, even when we do not agree, was clearly demonstrated by some of the psychological research carried out by Milgram. He managed to coerce fully grown adults into administering lethal doses of electric current to a 'student' for 'getting an answer wrong to a simple question' as part of 'some important research into learning'. The students, their cries of pain and silences, and the lethal currents were in fact fake. But the point is people were prepared to press the button even if it gave them considerable personal trauma. A child who is going to realise their full potential will need to be able to challenge power and authority appropriately.

Challenging authority

Authority has the task of creating and imposing rules for society that benefit the greater good against selfish self-interest. But not all rules are this altruistic. Some need challenging.

Being confident and internally referenced means that you do not allow yourself to be bullied into anything that you do not wish to do. So learning to challenge authority appropriately, to know the difference between valuable and pointless rules, is a central theme in childhood. Mostly challenging children are labelled 'difficult' because they make life harder for adults. They are saying 'your rules do not make sense, prove it'.

Society only makes progress when its norms and values are challenged. Authority needs challenging if it is to be effective. And we need to be able to do this constructively.

Try it now

Assess the power balance in the relationships around you by answering the following questions:

1 How much time do you spend reflecting on a request or comment from your child?
2 How quickly do you respond to your child's demands?
3 Do you give answers to requests without discussion?
4 Do you take time to consider how important this request is to your child?
5 Do you give your child full attention while discussing their request?
6 How effective are you at saying 'no' appropriately?

Answering questions like these is an opportunity for you to reflect and consider what you are currently doing and if this is or is not the intention that you have. With children over about seven years of age it might be interesting to ask them to answer these questions about you as a parent. Then you can see if your intentions are what is experienced by your child.

Learning by example

So far the idea that life is a process of continual learning has been explored at some length. To put this into practice we need to apply it specifically to the influences on a child in the context of the whole social environment. This is called 'socialisation', whereby a child learns the rules and how to fit in with the social environment in which it is born.

Understanding how society functions is learned by observing

those around us. The first role models we have are close family members. These behaviours get copied and mirrored back to us. The more people your child comes into contact with, the better range of role models they have to choose from. Childminders and extended family influences, nursery school teachers and peers all provide each child with a range of options. It is often possible to see one behaviour adopted from one source member and another from elsewhere. Equally the child is rejecting alternatives from everyone else. Thus children show discernment from a very early age. Each time a child rejects or adopts a behaviour pattern they are making a choice. As parents it is our role to guide our children into making the best choices whenever possible.

Imitating skills of young children

How often do we see ourselves through the eyes of our child, aspects that we prefer not to see? Mirroring is a wonderful opportunity to examine our own behaviours and take note of the model we are providing. If you dislike something that your child does it is probably because you dislike or fear something similar in yourself. How do you respond in these situations:

- Do you become angry or irritated by the child?
- Do you consider what this is telling you about yourself?
- Do you ignore them and hope it will go away?

It is pointless becoming angry with the child for their behaviour if you are the original model for them. If it is copied from someone else and you dislike it, consider why this is so. Make sure that it is not your own agenda influencing you. Discuss the influence and its merits with your child, and offer them alternatives so that they can make a choice of which role model to follow. Having found a comfortable one for themselves, they will adopt it as a model of their own behaviour patterns. Parents should seek to respect the unskilful choices of a child but support them in learning about their choice.

It can take some time to reprogramme behaviour, but is achievable once we have openly and honestly acknowledged our need to change.

> The most positive response a parent can give is to recognise the opportunity to change our own behaviour, and thereby provide a role model that our child can value and respect.

Parents often underestimate how much of an impression their own efforts to change make on their children. This provides an excellent role model because it gives children permission to try things out and make changes. The meta-message is **change is good.**

Fearing change

Fear of change is the biggest block to emotional competence. Yet work done in therapy and personal development does achieve change, to enhance the inner self and peel away the negative behaviours which are the result of fear. Many adults experience considerable fear of change and will resist it to quite extraordinary degrees, until the change is forced upon them painfully and dramatically – or they live a safe life that avoids challenges and achieves little. If your intention is to raise a successful child, then neither of these options will support that goal. Look back to Maslow's characteristics of self-actualisers (page 26) to see how many of these you hold.

Valuing children's mistakes

All children make mistakes. All adults make mistakes. Everyone fails to achieve something at first and it is the process of trying that allows us to succeed a few attempts down the line. Having also failed first, we know how to avoid further pitfalls. Failing first is essential for thorough learning to take place. Children need to have all their attempts valued, not just the successful ones. It is the process that counts, not the final outcome. If we only praise the successful outcome we undervalue the process it took to get there. Essential to success in professional, academic, social and emotional life is valuing the process and using it as a positive learning opportunity. By valuing it, we do not retreat from difficulty and remain open to the process of growth.

Recognising hidden agendas in parenting

Whether we like it or not, most people are experts in games of hidden agendas because most families play them to a degree. Such games vary enormously in severity and often follow the type of communication patterns of Jane, Megan and Keith (see pages 23 and 46). The main point here is that they all have a hidden or secondary gain other than the expressed intention and use dishonest communication styles and double binds. As with most aspects of parenting, in order to avoid teaching your child the same styles, you must look at your communication patterns and hidden agendas.

Using children to gain love

One of the fundamental needs for all humans is to feel loved but we can only receive that which we also give out. Keith needs love and uses his daughter and others to fulfil that need. He does not give love and receive it in return, he extracts it.

Babies are experts at giving out love, which they need to receive as care for survival. They are totally dependent on their parents, even if they are being abused. In order to receive, babies give unconditionally. They already know this rule and give endless uncritical and forgiving love. It has no hidden agendas. It is a means to survival as a human being and this is a fundamental truth for all of us.

Babies are born with this capacity and it is childhood experience that teaches them differently. If, as a parent, you already have unconditional love, why do you need to distort your child's love by manipulating it, like Megan and Keith?

> For everything in life, especially love, you receive what you give out and you give out what you have learned. Damaged love is still the best that a person can do if that is all they know.

If you have had a lack of love in your own childhood, your insecurity will make it hard for you to trust and rely on the lasting quality of the love from your child. If our emotional pot is empty, no matter how much love our child gives us, it will never be enough. Only we can learn how to fill it for ourselves.

Your need to be loved as a parent will create in your child a sense of failure. This is a totally limiting lesson for your child and is an example of unskilful choices on the part of the parents. But it can also change as soon as it is recognised.

Having favourites

Having favourites is even more destructive to the child concerned because of the pressure upon them to give the parent a reward in return for the position on the pedestal. The favoured child becomes isolated from siblings and locked into an impossible need fulfilment mission for the favouring parent. Who is taking care of the child's needs?

Using children to gain a sense of power

In much of our adult life we seem to have little power. As children this may feel even more true. There are always people who have more authority, more muscles, more money, more of whatever it is that appears to give them power. These are just illusions. True power comes from inner knowledge and strength, from a sense of integrity, knowing your boundaries, what you will and will not do, or allow others to do to you. It involves understanding that the bad behaviour of others is their responsibility and not yours and all your behaviour is your responsibility.

Case study: Megan _____

Megan is telling Keith that she wants to see Jane and Sam. This makes Keith very insecure and he expresses this as anger. Megan sees how distressed her father is and feels guilty about it. She decides not to see them any more. Keith then apologises to Megan and tells her not to talk about Jane and Sam any more because of how they have treated him. Megan is left feeling that she was wrong to bring up the subject. _____

Showing anger – losing control

If we as parents lose our temper and behave badly as a result, then justify this by indirectly telling the child they are to blame for having upset us, this is using the child to protect us from our own unresolved emotions. If we really want the best for our children then we must be prepared to heal our own hurts and take full responsibility for all our behaviours. We must learn to make skilful choices. Consider the outcome for the Fox (see Chapter 10). He was out of control with fear, in the form of anger, of things not going his way. He was not prepared to deal with his own fear and therefore his worst fears came true.

Consider this

The following is an excellent metaphorical account of the power of anger.

> There once was a little boy who had a bad temper. His father gave him a bag of nails and told him that every time he lost his temper, he must hammer a nail into the back of the fence. The first day the boy hammered 37 nails into the fence. Over the next few weeks, as he learned to control his anger, the number of nails hammered daily gradually dwindled down. He discovered it was easier to hold his temper than to drive those nails into the fence.
>
> Finally the day came when the boy didn't lost his temper at all. He told his father about it and the father suggested that the boy should now pull out one nail for each day that he was able to hold his temper. The days passed and the young boy was finally able to tell his father that all the nails were gone.
>
> The father took his son by the hand and led him to the fence. He said, 'You have done well, my son, but look at the holes in the fence. The fence will never be the same. When you say things in anger, they leave a scar just like this one. You can put a knife in a man and draw it out. It won't matter how many times you say I'm sorry, the wound is still there. A verbal wound is as bad as a physical one.'

Does this story make you think of any events in the past in your own life? Like all metaphorical stories, it can help us to understand our own behaviour more profoundly than the event itself.

Assertiveness skills

Parents need to be in charge and children need to feel secure and confident in the boundaries and rules that parents establish. So parents need to learn to say 'no' and to stick to it. This is discussed in more depth later on. But the biggest problem most parents have is a conflict between being nice and being a positive role model. Sometimes we have to be strong and accept that being a parent means saying 'no', means not being 'nice' all the time. It means setting strong rules and sticking to them.

Self-management and power

As parents we can wield power over our children in a number of ways:

◆ making decisions for them
◆ denying them the right to make mistakes
◆ making the feel guilty for upsetting us
◆ denying their right for a degree of autonomy in their own lives.

If we lack a sense of autonomy in our own lives, we feel powerless. One of the ways in which we can make ourselves feel more powerful is to use the models of power that other people use over us. If we do that then we are passing on our own sense of inadequacy to our child.

> We can never feel powerful in our own lives if we do not recognise our powerlessness first and acknowledge our strength in that honesty.

If we use our children's lives as an exercise in regaining the power in our own, we are abusing our children and teaching them that they too are powerless. By removing their sense of power we also remove their sense of potential and redirect the energy they need in order to achieve their goals into the desire to fill the need for autonomy in their lives.

Wanting to be god

Some parents try to be the superhuman, the ideal that they wish they could be and that perhaps their parents also created an illusion of. The trouble with being god is that eventually your child will notice that you are not and this will confuse, disillusion and ultimately undermine the very esteem and respect upon which their love is based.

In playing god you are also denying the child the right to be special in their own way. There can only be one god. However, they will probably spend the rest of their lives looking for someone to treat them like a god and fail at relationships because their ideals are too high and based on fear of not being god, of not being as good as their parents. The honest parent who makes honest mistakes teaches their child to love others as equal humans and most of all to love themselves as a less than perfect human. If we want to be god then we are also certainly feeling very inadequate inside and are struggling to hide it from everyone, including ourselves.

Using children to feel needed

In modern society the apprenticeship for adulthood lasts far longer than attaining adult physical status. The more complex a society is, the harder it is for the individual to be truly independent and indeed none of us are. We all need each other but there is a difference between dependency and interdependence. The latter is acceptable because it implies equality of dependency and working together for the greater good.

However, we all need to have our own sense of direction. Unfortunately many parents see their children's needs as their own identity, their value in society. If it is a choice to have children then allow the child to develop in their own direction. Deciding unilaterally what is best for your child is meeting your own needs for your child to show you up well in society, to enhance your social standing. Making sacrifices or staying at home to care for your children, and then demonstrating a lack of direction when they no longer need you, puts pressure on them to continue to be dependent. Children should never feel beholden to their parents. A relationship free from hidden agendas will allow the child to become all that they are, and create a healthy respect and affection to carry the relationship through into old age.

Summary

Parenting skills are so wide in range that it is impossible to list or describe them specifically. The important thing is to be the parent that reflects who you are, to develop the relationship between you and your child that will be good for both of you.

- ♦ Parenting skills are learned on the job but are also based on a range of influences. Awareness of these allows conscious choice.
- ♦ Our own childhood was the making of us and it is our responsibility to make that a positive outcome.
- ♦ Recognise the power roles in parenting and balance them for the child's developing sense of autonomy.
- ♦ Recognise the mirroring of ourselves by our children and use this as an opportunity to change.
- ♦ Accept the fact of hidden agendas in parenting and diffuse them through recognition and self-healing.

CHAPTER 5

The role of a parent is to teach a child how to care for themselves, to develop self-reliance and confidence.

Avoiding the Protection Trap

C hildhood is a special period of life. It has a certain precious quality because once it is gone it can never be repeated. However, it has a specific purpose. It is the apprenticeship for dealing with adult life, and like all good apprenticeships, there is a lot to learn. Physical survival is no longer the primary concern for parents. As pointed out by many child psychologists and philosophers, in the first half of this century parents wondered *if* their child would grow up. Now we worry about *how* our child will grow up.

Assessing the importance of making mistakes

Think about times that taught you the most important lessons in your own life, and the events that sparked off that greatest period of learning. I am talking about life lessons, the kind that teach you about other people, and most of all teach you about yourself. I expect most learning and advancement occurred, in terms of self-knowledge and knowledge of other people and life generally, at a time of great inner struggle. The most difficult experiences are amongst our best teachers, if we allow it. They are equally essential to continuing growth and development.

Try it now

What were the most important lessons that you learned in your life? List them, and then think about what kind of lessons they were. Try fitting them under each of the following headings:

love	creativity	joy
forgiveness	patience	compassion
prosperity	trust	responsibility
health	friendship	empathy
generosity	honesty	knowledge
respect	communication	intuition

These are the important lessons because they relate to other people and to our self-knowledge. If we accept the value of self-exploration, we teach our children to have a healthy outlook and sense of self. We can forgive and release negative experiences through exercises such as the inner child healing.

Work through the following questions and give yourself time to consider your responses:

- Was there any other way that you could have learned those lessons as thoroughly?
- Was there anyone who could have told you about those lessons and saved you the experience?
- Would you have listened?

Please answer these questions as you remember feeling **before** you went through the experience and before the wisdom and learning occurred. **Do not** use the wisdom of hindsight.

Learning lessons in six dimensions

Some lessons appear to be easier than others, but in reality they are not, for each lesson has to be learned in six dimensional approaches (see Figure 2). It cannot happen all at once. Each lesson is learned in a series of many little steps or a couple of big and very tough ones. The harder the lesson, the greater the potential for learning. 'No pain, no gain.' The more quickly we learn these lessons, the more quickly we advance in our emotional intelligence.

There are two choices for dealing with traumatic experiences.

1 The first is to become damaged, to see yourself as the victim, to retreat from any situation that might similarly challenge you. This is negative learning. It increases fear and life avoidance. It creates low self-esteem, failure and limitation.

2 The second is to see the positive in every situation, and use it to your advantage for increasing your self-awareness and inner peace. This is the best form of revenge because the persecutor has no power over you at all. Your life is wonderful regardless of their behaviour and because of yours.

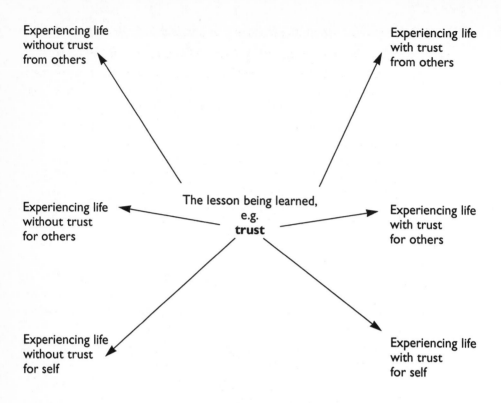

Fig. 2.   Directions of learning.

Try it now   Before continuing, answer 'yes' or 'no' to the following questions:

- Are there any areas of your life where the lessons were so hard that you have withdrawn to any degree from that part of your life?
- Have your withdrawals been temporary or permanent?
- Do you desire success in that area of your life regardless of the past?
- Do you feel confused by why it never seems to go right?
- Does someone else always seem to mess it up by not doing what you want them to do?

If your answers are 'yes' to any area in your life – and if we're at all honest there will be at least one area of our own lives where 'yes' is, in part at least, the truthful answer – then it is because you've still got lessons to learn.

Learning the lessons as they are presented to us

As adults, we frequently revisit experiences in different formats. Take one of the lessons such as trust. If there are six dimensions to learning a life lessons (see Figure 2), we have to learn each of them to fully understand and live with complete trust.

Case study: Jane _____

As a young girl Jane was repeatedly beaten by her father for being naughty. She didn't understand why because he never bothered to explain it to her. But she knew that her father was so big and she depended on him for everything so he must be right. She learned to try very hard to always get things right and to please her father. She learned two specific lessons:

♦ to associate love with fear
♦ no matter how hard you try, you will fail.

All through Jane's life, an aunt has developed a special relationship with her. This aunt showed the opposite kind of love, accepting, supporting and non-judgemental. She saw the positive sides to Jane's qualities and admired her for them. Jane was fond of her aunt but the relationship was not very regular because of distance. She was not a significant influence in Jane's early life.

As Jane grew older she learned that her father might actually be wrong. She also realised that her father was scared of being wrong. This gave her a sense of power over him, a redress of the unfair balance of power she experienced as a young girl. As she reaches adulthood she learns that she can use guilt and fear to make her father give her what she wants. He can't hit her any more but he can now use money to keep her love. Jane then meets a man and marries. After the first three years her husband hits her for challenging him. He feels guilty and begs forgiveness. Jane forgives him and he takes her out to buy some new clothes. She can choose whatever she likes. They agree to have a child and she falls pregnant._____

The cycle continues. Jane has not learned the lessons of her childhood experiences and is stuck in the same pattern of behaviour and response until she can learn all the lessons from the negative side.

What I have noticed, from both personal and professional experience, is that there is almost always a counter example available to us if we choose to see it. Jane has an aunt who is showing a much more positive attitude and expression of love, but Jane is too locked into the battle with her father to take much notice of it. Once we develop the ability to step back from life and notice what we are being shown we can start to see the counter examples, the demonstrations of more skilful behaviour and more effective choices in life.

We cannot understand love and trust until we have learned to be without it, and we cannot understand the full value of living without fear until we have lived with it. It is the negative side that teaches us the full value of the positive side. One type of lesson is not better than another and all experiences are lessons. But we can so easily overlook the examples of the positive side if we are locked into battles of power and victimhood.

Accepting the lessons

Commonly, people who experienced a traumatic or violent childhood will repeat those experiences and find similar adult partners. If they haven't fully explored the experiences of that childhood with an open and gentle learning approach, they will not have learned the lessons they need.

If we had experience of parenting similar to that described above (Jane's father), or a variation, we can choose to learn from that experience.

- We can choose how not to parent using fear as a control over our children's love for us.
- We can learn from the mistakes of our parents and those traumatic experiences in a very important way because we know exactly how it feels to live with that kind of parenting.
- We have the choice, to continue to live like that ourselves or to choose an alternative.

Protecting or inhibiting

The important thing about difficult experiences is not who is right or wrong, who hurt who and so on. The important thing is the learning we receive. By being denied difficult experiences, a child cannot test their strength, learn and understand in their own way. You are denying them learning in their early years. This means they inevitably experience the repeating pattern later, when you are not responsible as a parent. But their ability to handle and manage their adulthood is undermined.

> If you, as a parent, put off the lesson for your child, it will be learned later and possibly with more traumatic or longer-lasting consequences, especially if they haven't got the coping skills that childhood should have provided them with.

If you're not providing your child with challenging experiences within the family, they will have to face the challenges somewhere else.

Play and freedom – how much is safe?

This is an issue for parents every day after school, and at weekends, but especially during the long summer holidays. If your children are like mine were, they also probably want to go off with their friends and not spend the holidays with you all the time. So how much freedom do children need and what is safe?

Childhood is an apprenticeship for adult life, so what sort of adult do you want your child to become? Do you want them to be timid and uncertain about taking risks in life, cautious and as a result missing out on the fullness of experience and opportunity that life can offer? Of course, all children have their own unique personalities and some are obviously more adventurous than others. We need to be different because if everyone wanted to go off and explore the world, there would be no one at home. It is more to do with self-confidence and being able to challenge within the negative counterpart – fear.

Adventure and safety

The way we approach life will affect our children's approach to life. If we live timidly then our children will learn to be fearful as adults too.

What has freedom in the holidays got to do with confidence? Allowing your child to go off on their own gives them a chance to see what they can do for themselves. It gives them a chance to interact with the adult world and see how they cope. At times they will get into a pickle but the important thing is to accept their need to make mistakes and learn from them. It is too easy as a parent to give way to our own fears of what might happen and

how we would live with ourselves if the 'what if' did actually
occur. But we may actually be harming our child by protecting
them too much from finding their own strength and coping
strategies.

Perspectives on 'the world out there'

Protecting your child is natural and part of the role of a parent. It
is essential. But it is very easy to view the world out there as 'a big
nasty place, peopled with perverts and dangerous drivers'. Yet
statistically speaking your child is at far greater risk of injury or
abuse within your own home and family, as any social services
department will confirm. The only group of people at more risk
of violence against them outside the home than within is teenage
boys.

If we say 'no' to a request to go to the park with friends or
alone, 'no adults', we are communicating several hidden messages:

1   You do not trust them or their ability to cope. But if you do
    not trust them, how can they learn to trust themselves? They
    may feel it is not worth being trustworthy if you do not trust
    them in the first place – they have nothing to live up to.
2   You do not trust your own parenting skills, you have not
    taught them what they need to know in order to be safe out
    there. If you don't trust you, then how can they feel secure
    trusting you as a role model?
3   The world is a place to be scared of and other people are not to
    be trusted, it is not safe out there for anyone. But they are also
    part of that world out there at times, so how should they
    behave? Does that mean that they become untrustworthy by
    being out there too?

Body language reflecting inner beliefs

There has been a lot of research into what makes a bully, mugger
or rapist select one victim and not another, but most of it is to do
with body language. A mugger can instinctively pick up non-
verbal clues as to the mental perspective of the potential victim:

◆   Do they have a victim mentality?
◆   Will they fight or yield?

- Will I get what I want out of this approach?

They can read us in an instant and usually quite unconsciously. But they will get it right 99 per cent of the time. So if we want to protect our child, the best thing we can do is to teach them:

- to have greater confidence in how safe it is out there
- how the odd distorted people do exist but it is possible to deal with them
- that they have nothing to fear if they are sensible and make safe, self-valuing choices for themselves.

There is a lot of psychological research into why people get easily led and the answer is because they fear authority and do not believe they have the right to say no to adults/superiors. We must teach them. An educated, self-aware child will not be persuaded to do something against their instincts for their own good. But an insecure and timid child is easy and a naive, innocent one is almost as vulnerable. Teaching children to go out and feel confident that anything coming their way will be possible to deal with will give them the right body language, which means that they will not get picked in the first place.

Media-perpetuated beliefs

In the final analysis, whom are we really protecting if we say 'no' too often? If we are honest it is not our child; it is our self, the parent who does not want to take a chance with 'what ifs'. In the end we are all doing the best we can with what we know and parenting is one of the hardest roles we ever take on, but stop and think about what your real motives are when you prefer to keep your children supervised at all times. Life is not really more dangerous than it was 50 or 100 years ago. It is only our perception that it is. This is a result of the media. Being informed does not have to mean becoming scared or avoiding life. It does mean offering information so you can continue to explore all that life offers but with a greater level of awareness of the unexpected happening. And with greater resources to cope, if and when it does happen.

As long as you are aware of why you make the decision that you do make and are aware of whom you are really wanting to protect, then whatever you will decide will be the best you can do as a parent. In the end we never know what might or would have happened, only what does.

Case study: Jane and Sam _____

Jane has started working again after leaving her violent ex-husband. She enjoys the work and tells Sam, a twelve-year-old boy, that he must travel home from school alone. This is fine for eight months and he enjoys the freedom. One day he is attacked, as he gets off the bus near his home, by a gang of slightly older boys from his school. He is physically injured, mostly cuts and bruises, and is shaken by the experience. Jane is upset and shocked. She feels guilty that she enjoys working and made him travel alone. She hushes him whenever he starts to show he is upset. She tells him that it was all wrong, that people shouldn't treat him like that and he didn't deserve it. It will never happen again.

The physical injuries heal quickly. She rearranges her work time to allow her to leave a little earlier. From now on she collects him either from school or from the bus stop every day, to make sure that it will never happen again and to show her son how much she loves him. She tells herself and everyone else that she is protecting her adolescent son from the possibility of this recurring. _____

- ◆ Whom is Jane protecting and from what?
- ◆ How does Sam feel when faced by a similar experience inside the school grounds?
- ◆ What lessons has Sam learned from this experience?
- ◆ Is Jane protecting her son from the possibility of an attack or herself from the guilt she feels from his first attack?

Jane feels that somehow she should have protected him and it shouldn't have happened. He shouldn't have been exposed to that violence.

Why not? All through life we are on the receiving end of attacks from other people. Sometimes they are physical and sometimes they are verbal, emotional, psychological or spiritual. Our response to them is also a matter of choice.

- ◆ How do we deal with them – looking for the learning or feeling fearful and angry?
- ◆ Are we injured by them, become a victim, feeling 'poor me, it's not fair'?
- ◆ Or do we see them as a result of someone else's problem?

There are many ways of coping with assaults on our integrity whether they are physical or psychological. But without experiences, we do not know what our coping skills are. We do not know how to survive and we become damaged.

Sam's physical cuts and bruises only took a couple of weeks to heal but the emotional healing will take much longer unless it is addressed as an opportunity to learn from. If Jane feels guilty about 'letting it happen', she will transfer that guilt on to Sam. But he will understand that he caused his mother's guilt, therefore accepting responsibility. He feels ashamed of the assault, and is not allowed to talk about it. Somehow he must have been asking for it.

◆ What coping skills has Sam been able to develop?

Sam has probably learned 'Let someone else deal with the problem and protect me'. Is this a lesson of any use at all? Will this enable Sam to deal with other forms of attack later in life? It's important not to become judgemental here but to allow that we, as parents, are also allowed to make mistakes and learn our lessons. As discussed earlier, children tend to respect their parents *more* for not 'being right' all the time.

◆ What would you feel if it were your child?
◆ What would you automatically want to do?
◆ Whose needs would you be addressing?
◆ Whose needs should you really be addressing?

There are no mistakes, only lessons to be learned. It would be a good idea to introduce this as a daily pause for thought for everyone. We would all make progress in our lives if we were not so afraid of learning lessons by getting it wrong first.

Putting off the lessons

Jane is putting off the lessons for Sam to learn. Many people would think it best under the circumstances. What would any of us do in similar circumstances with our own children? There is much evidence, especially on street rape and assault, that it is less likely to happen to people who walk confidently. The rapist or bully does not enjoy the violence as much as they want the sense of power for boosting their own sense of powerlessness. By preventing your child from being confident in themselves and undermining their ability to cope, you place them at greater risk:

- Is Jane really protecting Sam from the chance of another attack or is she increasing the likelihood?
- How is Sam's self-concept and perception developing: victim or independent young man?
- What other choices are there for dealing with a situation like this?
- What choices are you currently making for your children?

How could a parent teach a child to learn from this kind of experience?

Such an experience can undermine self-esteem but there are ways this can be approached.

- Help the child to face their fear of a recurrence by looking at what the experience has already taught them.
- What were their emotional reactions as the experience progressed? Discuss in depth exactly how everything that happened affected them and talk it through. Nothing is unacceptable.
- Help them recognise the lessons.
- Teach them about the victim/bully system.

Using experiences positively

This sort of experience can be an excellent opportunity to teach an important lesson in empathy. Being on the receiving end of violence may be something that they will need to think about. In the future if they are tempted to attack someone, this experience reminds them what it feels like at the other end.

- Would they want to make someone feel like they feel?
- If they ever lose their temper, that can be what it feels like on the other side.
- What might it feel like for someone else whom they observe being bullied?

Managing what you can and leaving the rest

You cannot control the environment and other people. You cannot control the experiences your child may or may not have. Any fear you feel from your desire to and inability to control the world out there will transfer to your child as guilt, shame and low self-esteem. This is the damage, not the incident itself. Victims of assault are encouraged to discuss their experiences, being open about what happened, not endlessly talking in terms of feeling angry towards the people who assaulted them, and ideas of revenge.

Protection creates bigger problems

Protecting your child too much can actually make it twice as hard for them to learn from the lesson when it returns next time because they will still have to release the fear and shame from the earlier incident. It is never easier to learn the lessons later in life. It just means there is far more work to do and there is far more potential wasted. The more deeply embedded an emotional experience is within us, the more power it has to hurt us in all other areas of our life.

> Identifying yourself as a survivor of abuse is another way of perpetuating that abuse. Freeing yourself from the identity and effects of that abuse on your own life is taking back the power.

The perpetrators also have their pain and their lessons to learn, possibly more than the victim. They also need to heal and be treated with compassion. They also need acceptance as human beings.

Reinforcing the positive

If your child has experienced an assault of some kind, however minor, acknowledge that whatever they feel is OK. Their feelings are valid. And immediately give them reasons to feel good about themselves. Look at what they did get right:

◆ not retaliating and behaving exactly as their persecutors did

◆ not giving the bullies an excuse to become more aggressive
◆ not allowing the bullies to gain total power over them by giving into their demands if there were any.

What we usually fail to remember is that the bullies are often victims of bullying and their behaviour is usually a reflection of their treatment elsewhere. The bullying child is also a hurting child and the only way they have of feeling any power in their own lives is to exercise it over others as it is exercised over them. If your child is on the receiving end of bullying, don't turn them into a bigger victim, help them to understand the process and, with support, to work it through for themselves.

> People who feel good about themselves do not need to behave in ways that threaten, injure or are unkind to others. They have self-acceptance and therefore acceptance of others.

Parents who are afraid teach their child to live with fear

Fear is part of being human. It is our warning to care for ourselves. It is essential for our protection but it must not become over-protective. Too much fear and we never take a chance in our lives, never explore our potential and self-actualise. There are many examples where the consensus of fear curtails lives. For instance, women who are afraid to go out at night are passing on the message of fear and of 'woman as victim' to both sons and daughters. All emotions attract like to themselves. The more fearful we are, the more likely we are to be attacked either physically or emotionally.

◆ By using fear to protect your children from attack, what are you teaching them?
◆ What is more likely to occur later in life?
◆ When you protect your child, whom are you really protecting?
◆ What voices are you listening to?
◆ What lessons are you all learning and what lessons are you avoiding or missing opportunities for?

The inner voices that guide us

Freud was one of the first people to formally acknowledge the inner voices. He called these the 'internalised parent' and placed them in an area of personality called the Superego.

According to Freud, this was not fully developed until around age 5–6. This is the age at which children are able to make moral judgements of their own. As parents we are all still responding to our own inner voices as well as presenting our child with their own set. These remain in the subconscious unless we change them. If you are truly honest in the questions above, if your own voices of fear, guilt and shame, that you are lacking as a parent for not protecting your child, are coming through loud and clear, you are over-protecting your own child and passing on to them the same legacy. The consensus from most parents would be that they would do anything to protect their child and this makes us believe this is the right thing to do. These ideas are challenging and a little confrontational but can you allow yourself to see the value in their argument and let go of your own fear?

Case Study: Jane_____

Jane is a single mother with a teenage son, Sam. She has a reasonable living and enough money to go out from time to time. She likes to walk rather than drive and walks home alone at night. Sam sees her confident and safe, in control of her life, relaxed and comfortable with her mobility in the community. She is sometimes warned by well-meaning friends to be careful but she is confident that nothing will happen to her. She does not take unnecessary risks and is careful but will not allow her life to be curtailed by fear. _____

- ◆ What message is Jane giving Sam about women? What is he learning?
- ◆ What message is she giving Sam about fear?
- ◆ What is she continuing to learn from her own experience?

If a woman displays fear of other males, the message that she is giving to her son is that when he is adult, he will be a 'possible risk'. So young boys learn their potential as a source of terror as they are forming their self-concept. This will encourage the development of a fear of themselves and their potential, an immediate block to finding love and companionship. It may encourage them to use fear as a way of gaining a sense of power in life but it will not bring out their full potential. Fear, in its many guises, is the emotion that prevents achievement. The meta-messages we give children about other adults contribute to their development of a sense of the self they will become.

Welcoming the lessons

We have fully learned all that there is to understand about an experience when we can actually look at the experience and be completely and fully glad that it happened.

If Jane gets to the point in her life when she recognises her association of love and violence, and heals her attraction to power games, she can thank her father, husband and Keith for all they taught her and welcome the experience. She will be able to accept that she needed to go through that experience in order to learn. It is one of the most important positive areas of her life because it was her greatest teacher and will bring her to an inner freedom that she could not have appreciated properly without that learning.

She can now be discerning and choose not to engage in a similar experience again. You can't appreciate something you've got if you don't know what it is like to be without it. That rule applies to both material and emotional growth. That is the learning we need to achieve for ourselves as parents and to lead our children towards. When Jane and Sam can look back and be glad that he experienced the attack because of the learning they have both gained from the experience, this will bring them closer. The alternative is setting up a guilt/fear barrier which neither will want and will overcome through dependency in order to feel secure, to maintain the sense of closeness.

Case study: Jane _____

Jane was repeatedly patronised and criticised by her mother, Mary. She was also not protected by her mother from her father's beatings. In fact she saw her mother as causing many of the beatings with her criticisms. She grew up feeling angry with her mother, unable to believe that Mary loved her. This made her determined to prove her mother wrong and Jane lived with the anger of that rejection for part of her adult life. It wasn't until she had achieved quite a lot in her career, but had been unable to maintain a steady relationship, that she sought counselling. With help she was able to value the lessons that Mary had taught her and heal the anger. She realised, when she stopped being angry with Mary, that she had learned to become very strong and self-reliant. Then she was able to find happiness and be grateful for all her lessons. Although it took her years to learn, the future just got better after that. _____

Summary

This chapter has explored the ways in which parents can facilitate the learning of lessons and not fall into the trap of protecting their children from too much of life, creating fear-based adults who are less likely to realise their potential in life. This involves:

- ◆ Recognising the importance of learning from real life when it happens, not avoiding and putting off learning until later on.
- ◆ Prioritising a child's need to gain self-confidence over a need to protect yourself from your own fear.
- ◆ Recognising and taking full responsibility for all your experiences in life and teaching your child to do the same.
- ◆ Supporting the learning of lessons in a positive and progressive way that encourages self-awareness and self-esteem.

The only true discipline is self-discipline, knowing exactly why you will, or will not, behave in a particular way.

Disciplining or Devastating Your Child?

Discipline, and how we approach it, is a key factor in teaching your child to feel free to develop their whole potential or to hold limitation beliefs. It is one of the most important areas of life because it is our responsibility to teach our children to make skilful choices for themselves and to avoid certain types of experiences if possible for their own good. But it is also one of the areas which leads to all forms of emotional and physical abuse, sometimes with seriously disastrous outcomes in the long term.

Assessing the purpose of discipline

Discipline is not something done for its own sake. It has a purpose and is our response to a behaviour from our child. We talk of discipline with a clear intention of what we hope to achieve in our parental role, don't we. Or do we? What exactly do you intend as the outcome of your response, your disciplinary treatment of your child?

My dictionary defines discipline as:

◆ maintenance of order and obedience amongst pupils, subordinates, etc.
◆ corrective punishment
◆ a system of rules and punishments.

Try it now

What does discipline mean to you? What is the outcome you wish to achieve when you discipline your child? How much thought have you given to this question?

◆ Is your intention similar to the above dictionary definition? Which part?
◆ Is discipline intended to prevent your children coming to harm?
◆ Is it intended to make your life as parents easier?

◆ Is it intended to teach your children not to repeat a behaviour/action?

◆ Is it intended to teach them to do something differently?

◆ Is it intended to help them understand many different ways of doing things, of speaking and acting?

◆ Is it intended to enable them to recognise the consequences of their own actions for themselves and for others (without guilt)?

Exploring ideas about discipline

In our approaches to discipline, we need to examine whether we are facilitating our child in their learning, or making it harder for them in the long run in order to make it easier for ourselves in the short term. The trouble is that most of us do not really think about this area of parenting with enough reflection on the long-term consequences of our policies. Many parents even use the defensive argument that 'if it was good enough for me it is good enough for them'.

1   This is denying any difficulties you may have felt at the time or are experiencing now.

2   There is no perfect parent, there never has been and there never will be.

3   Parents all make mistakes and this is good for children to learn from, for making better choices.

4   Everyone has a personal area of difficulty at some level, unless you have reached full enlightenment about the state of being human.

5   Perpetuating your experiences is another way of expressing your pain, in the only way you know how, by inflicting them on your child.

6   Realising both your own and your child's potential requires that you stop being afraid to self-examine and re-address your own childhood experiences.

'Experts' offer many conflicting opinions about the right way to discipline children. This chapter incorporates points already covered earlier in the book and breaks down the arguments. Then you can make your own choices, of what is best for you in your role as a parent.

Attitudes to discipline

Our attitude to discipline is based on a range of smaller ideas that we collect in order to gain our understanding of the overall concept. These ideas:

- are based on concepts of good and bad, right and wrong
- do not accept the possibility of learning from everything that happens, all the mistakes that we make
- overlook the fact that no one gets it right all the time
- are based on judgement and criticism of other people
- ignore the fact that all criticism and judgement of others is always based on what we feel or believe about ourself
- are based on a fear of being wrong as parents through the behaviour of our children now
- are based on a lack of acceptance of each unique quality or trait that is being explored and developed from all six dimensions.

There is no compassion available for being wrong, only fear in the recipient or observer, us the parent, that makes us respond with criticism and judgement. Empathy is ignored. Remembering our own mistakes as children and the fear of having been wrong, and remembering being criticised and punished then, we pass these fears on to our own children.

Recognising a need to take action

We know the things that are less skilful, in our own behaviour or our children's behaviour, or we are discovering them. Hopefully we are acknowledging the need to think about such behaviour and move on. We are consciously aware of what we need to do and roughly where we are going. We are not as confused any more. And that is what is important about always using the positive approach to all qualities. There is no point in using violence, fear, guilt or shame as a means of disciplinary action on our part. They are all very easy to manipulate and use as weapons of control against people. If you know someone is easily made to feel guilty, it is very easy to use this weapon. Have you ever used it, ever had it used against you?

Until we let go of the idea of 'wrong' it will carry on being in our lives. But, like the shadow, we can turn the light on and recognise that we no longer need to have it.

Challenging society's assumptions

The definition of discipline given above includes the word 'punishment'. Should we even consider using this word in relationship to children, especially young children? Yet the attitude is widespread in society that:

◆ 'If parents disciplined their children properly, society would have fewer problems.'

◆ 'If school teachers still used corporal punishment in school, we would not have problems with discipline and disruption in classrooms, etc.'

> Whenever ideas are presented as 'common sense', this is a warning that we are accepting ideas without discernment. Parents should examine these assumptions and recognise their appeal – and their danger.

As adults we should challenge every assumption we are given and question its meta-message. Throughout history, progress and change occurred because the social rules, values and assumptions were challenged. If we do not challenge and confront rules we do not make progress as a society.

By exploring each value and assumption, we can extract whatever we need to teach our children. Thus children are learning:

◆ how to make choices
◆ which rules to adhere to
◆ exactly why they are doing so.

Using what parents are getting right already as a basis, and keeping an open mind, we continue to learn and provide our children with a role model for learning which allows them to make successful choices.

Assessing smacking

There is a great debate over the use of smacking with children. Where do you draw lines? When it is reasonable control over your child and when does it become abusive? Children who experience physical assault on their person experience deep fear and humiliation. When is a smack also physical assault?

Try it now

This is an exercise in empathy:

- Think of a time recently when you made a mistake or got something wrong, accidentally broke something or otherwise behaved in a way that would not be considered socially acceptable.
- Imagine a giant who is at least twice your size coming into your room, and shouting at you with a very loud voice.
- Now imagine that person hitting you and it hurts.

Now answer these questions:

- What emotions are you experiencing?
- Do you like this person?
- Do you feel that your action justified this assault?
- What have you learned from this experience?

What was your response to this exercise? Did you think that you would feel good about the experience? Chances are that you disliked this experience. Children will feel a range of emotions and need to protect themselves against the fear and humiliation which is raised. There are two ways commonly used, or frequently a confused combination of both:

1 They can be angry with their parents and blame them for the problem, saying that they are wrong. Parents aren't gods and it is all their fault.
2 Children want their parents to be the good guys, to be people that they can be proud of, 'this is my mum/dad'. When we let them down, we let ourselves down too. To accommodate this idea that parents cannot be wrong, the child may say, 'Well I must be wrong, I must be a very bad person if my mum or dad thinks I deserve to be hurt this much.'

There are powerful meta-messages here, so discipline needs to be considered and applied with great care.

Invading boundaries

A **boundary** is a psychological or physical protection that maintains our sense of integrity and wholeness. They develop with a strong sense of self-esteem and personal knowledge. They are flexible and enable us to discern between relevant and irrelevant assaults on our person, physical or psychological. Boundaries allow us to live our lives successfully and confidently.

Barriers are defence mechanisms which also protect. They are rigid and work from a position of fear. They are very effective in preventing us achieving any goals.

Our body is precious to us and exclusive to us. People who invade that boundary are abusive. It is a form of rape in as much as the damage rape causes is less from the sexual act and more from the violation of the individual and their sense of personal space and integrity. Smacking, or even the threat of smacking, is an assault on the individual and their boundary, their territory.

There are two reasons why all smacking and threats are abusive:

1 Smacked children are less able to develop boundaries in adult life which allow people to be close to them in a safe way, the basis of any successful relationship. It leads people to learn that abuse and love go together and will either behave like that to a partner or allow behaviour like that towards themselves. It forms part of their unconscious belief system, even if consciously they reject it. The smack itself may last minutes in terms of physical hurt. The actual damage that can be done to a child's self-esteem, to their sense of safety and well-being, and their right to feel safe and protected, can be very long lasting.

2 The more often this kind of discipline is used, the less effective it becomes. The damage is longer-lasting, deeper and creates barriers instead of boundaries. This leads to a lack of self-discipline. Boundaries are explored in greater depth in the next chapter.

Avoiding shame and guilt

These two emotions are the biggest cause of under-performance, limitation beliefs and lack of emotional competence. Negative learning experiences through guilt and shame result in a child:

- feeling guilt or embarrassment for being wrong
- not understanding the value of getting it wrong
- learning the fear of getting it wrong
- feeling it is them who is wrong rather than something which they have done
- becoming inhibited about all learning for the future.

As the parent you have:

- made your role as parent more difficult for this particular situation
- created a situation where learning will become more difficult
- created resistance to admitting a mistake in the first place so preventing learning occurring
- created resistance to all learning, all change, all personal development within the child.

It is openness to change, the ability to cope with difficulty and ride the ups and downs, the niggles and hassles of life, that characterises the emotionally competent individual.

Consider this

'Shame and guilt are noble emotions that are essential in the maintenance of a civilised society and vital for the development of some of the most refined and elegant qualities of human potential: generosity, service, self-sacrifice, unselfishness and duty' (Willard Gaylen).

- Do you agree or disagree with this statement?
- Do you need to be made to feel ashamed and guilty in order to learn generosity?

Freewill or control?

The intention behind most of the times that you are feeling ashamed and guilty is to make you become something that you are not, but it is a coercion, it is a control. So if you are generous, you are not generous from the heart and with freedom, but because that is what you have got to do, because otherwise you are going to be ashamed. Are true generosity, and other desirable behaviours, actually true if only done through gritted teeth and with a sense of shame?

Using guilt and shame as a means of coercion, a form of humiliation to stop people from doing things, is not the way to get them to stop doing things. They have to decide 'this is not what I want to do' and they have to decide that with everything. It has to be a freewill choice. We can say to ourselves, 'I will not do that again because I don't wish to behave in this way, because I don't like the way it makes me feel, and I don't like what it does to other people. But it is my choice. No one is making me feel guilty about it, no one is making me ashamed of what I have done in the past, when I have done this act. I am not fearful, just making that choice.'

The approach we need to take is to accept the need to learn lessons. This releases us from the fear of who we were and what we did, which is gone, and we know that who we will be and who we are now is someone that we are comfortable with. Someone we don't need to feel ashamed or guilty about because we have changed. So we should start being aware that these forms of negative emotion make you do things that are not your choice. Sometimes the choices are quite good in that they make us behave in a way that is socially acceptable. But quite often these emotions make us act in a way that is against our own sense of self and that is where it starts becoming very unhealthy. The same mechanism can be used to make us do things that are unskilful and self-damaging, to make foolish choices like taking drugs and putting ourselves at risk.

The only guilt we need ever feel is when we are not being true to ourselves. It is very important to know what is right for you and not be coerced into doing things that other people want you to do.

Choice and freewill

If you choose to act happily and freely, there is no guilt attached, no manipulation. If you were given a choice to do this or not to do it and you would prefer not to but say 'OK, I'll still do it', that is a volitional action, there is no guilt attached to it. So if someone asks you to do something and you say 'Yes, I would be delighted to', and you mean it, then that is fine. But if you think, 'Well, I don't want to do this, but I had better say yes because if I don't I will look like a real maggot or something', that is not fine.

Do it because you want to, or don't do it, and be honest about what you want or don't want to do in any situation. Be true to yourself. Once you are true to yourself, you no longer feel guilt or shame.

Be compassionate with yourself. Next year you will be different. You're doing your best at the moment so do not punish yourself with these emotions or by hanging on to a belief in them.

Giving and receiving respect

Society expects children to be self-disciplined and motivated, yet shows little respect for them, little consideration for their needs for safety and room to play, develop and learn, and little consideration for the examples we set our children in society. The following points are so obvious and so rarely considered in any depth:

- Why should children respect adults when adults generally do not respect children?
- If we fail to respect children, on what basis can they learn to respect themselves or anyone else?
- What do they experience and learn about respect if they are learning to live without it?

Children learn to distrust the concept of respect, to consider that there must be a hidden agenda, a hidden motive, that nothing can be taken at face value, 'so why is this person treating me with respect, what do they want?'

> If we cannot feel respect for others and for ourselves and from others for ourselves, how can we project respect to others?

The mirroring principle holds true for society just as much as it does for individuals. The fact that so many children have little respect for others in society is the mirror being shown for society to take a good look at itself.

As parents we cannot change others – we can only change ourselves. By projecting respect you receive it. The more you respect your child and note their wonderful qualities, the more you will be appreciated, respected and listened to. It is so simple and yet so hard because we as adults need to work on ourselves in order to pass this message on to our children.

Learning styles for parents

If your children are 'naughty', ask yourself:

◆ What is that telling me about myself?

not

◆ What is it telling me about them?

Looking inwards is usually the hardest thing to do but there are ways in which we can do this if we want the best for our child. Focusing on them is transferring the responsibility for ourselves onto them. With that goes all the pressure and burden we are carrying, but doubled for our child. We cannot expect our children to address their behaviour if we do not address our own.

Applying rules

Parental hypocrisy is a damaging experience for a child. It teaches them to do as others say, not as they do. Parents who give a rule and fail to follow it themselves are undermining their own authority. Their child has every moral and reasonable right to challenge on that behaviour. If the parent feels threatened and makes this a disciplinary issue, they are compounding the negative experience for the child and obliterating the possibility of positive learning. It is important to make sure that any decisions made are backed up by your own behaviour. What we actually do and what we want to do can differ as long as we recognise this and accept the hypocrisy, but if our children are to learn from us they must respect us, faults and all.

Confusing fear and respect

Many people confuse fear with respect. With all due consideration it is easy to see that they are not the same, but if we have learned that they go together, they become connected on an internal emotional perceptual level.

Fear:

◆ prevents us from behaving in certain ways that attract punishment
◆ teaches avoidance of punishment
◆ prevents learning and understanding
◆ does not teach about the behaviour or act as any form of prevention in a real sense because the individual thinks that if they can do this and not get caught then this is all that matters
◆ teaches 'if I can get away with it, then I can do it'.

Children and adults taught from fear are acting without understanding fully why they should not behave in this way.

> The fear of getting caught can become a motivation because it releases adrenaline into our bodies, causing a state of arousal that is exciting and can be addictive.

For young males this is a way of testing their bravery and social status as a male. This may explain why crime amongst males is much higher than amongst females (although female crime rates are rising). They all want to 'feel the fear and do it anyway'. If discipline teaches avoidance of the negative outcome which can be avoided in another way, then they will. This is the simple basis for most anti-social behaviour.

> If we punish in conventional terms, we perpetuate the wrong lesson, the lesson that does not bring an understanding of why they should not want to behave like that for themselves and their own self-respect.

If the individual thinks that they can get away without being caught, they will continue. There is no understanding of why not to behave like this and no self-esteem boundaries. This scenario reflects the lack of respect for and from society for many individuals, the mirroring effect mentioned earlier. Discipline should be very much a case of do as you would be done by.

Positive discipline

Positive discipline is about helping your child to explore what it was that actually happened.

- They may well feel bad anyway and do not need it amplified by your reactions.
- They may well already feel stupid and unable to believe that they did that.

As a parent you have the power to heal and facilitate the learning. Debunk the actual thoughts and feelings by working through a list of questions, all of which avoid the dreaded **why**, which requires the individual to justify their actions and blocks any learning potential. Try this out on yourself first.

Try it now   Think of something you did that was a mistake and work through the following list of questions:

- What were your thoughts before doing this action?
- What did you hope to achieve with this action?
- What outcome did you achieve?
- How do these differ?
- What could you do differently if the same situation occurs again?
- What learning has occurred for your benefit?
- Is there any other way you could have learned such a valuable lesson?

Run through this exercise with your child and summarise the learning. Make them feel good for being honest and open to learning, praise them for their perception.

This lengthy and rather tedious process will develop its own shorthand form once you get used to the technique. You can support your child by:

- Helping your child analyse their thoughts and feelings prior to and during the offending behaviour. You enable them to learn and understand the experience fully.
- Saying that's OK and asking them what they can learn from what has happened. If they feel fear, remove the negative emotion which will block their learning and remind them that we all make mistakes and all learn from experience.

We cannot undo the past, ever, much as we might like to. Rather we need to use the past constructively for learning to get it right next time. This positive approach releases the fear immediately because a positive attitude will always override a negative one if you work with it. It allows healing and prevents a build-up of guilt, shame and fear which result in poor emotional and physical health in adulthood. Most importantly it facilitates learning.

Changing ideas about discipline

The approach outlined above is very different from the one assumed as effective in most discussions about disciplining children. It is more demanding on parents to begin with because they have to learn their way through the style and work on their own emotional responses to do with learning and being open to their own mistakes. It is never too late to start this approach and work on it, and don't worry if you get it wrong. Be open and discuss this with your child too: you may be surprised at their reaction to your honesty.

The final part of learning and disciplining is to value that mistake. Don't see a mistake, see an opportunity for learning and honour it. See making mistakes as something to be welcomed but not repeated. This requires a very clear boundary of accepting the behaviour and working with it. Any negative connotations will leave a residue of fear in some shape or form and that will require them to hide from the learning in order to escape from the negative feeling.

Recognising causes of anger

When we become angry with our children, it is because they have reflected something back to us which we do not like to acknowledge in ourselves, or we fear for ourselves, or in ourselves as parents. This makes us feel vulnerable and threatened, often at a subconscious level. Our response to our child is anger, as if they have done something wrong. They will not understand this. So not only are they confused as to what they have done wrong but they are then scared of an angry adult who is much bigger and more powerful than them. Is this the way to create respect between you and your child? Even jokey threats such as 'don't make me angry, you won't like me when I'm angry', lines from the incredible hulk or other such disguises, mean that you are still being angry and intimidating.

Using empathy again, how would you feel if someone at least twice your size came and started shouting at you or even suggesting that they might start shouting at you.

- Would you feel friendly and relaxed with that situation?
- Would you be able to listen and communicate easily?
- Would you feel open to learning something about yourself that requires you to admit you made a mistake?
- If you had no idea what you have done wrong, would you feel good about the person in front of you?
- Would you feel very insecure and full of fear?

Remember that our children are also our teachers and we should respect the lessons they teach us as much as we expect them to respect the lesson we teach them.

If you feel angry do not look at your child, look at yourself and ask what it is that you do not like to see mirrored back to you. Be honest, in the way that you want your child to be. Even discuss this with your child. Their clarity and openness often enables them to see the real truth more easily than adults who clutter it up with self-justification and complicated explanations that act as a mask to hide behind. We call this being adult, and understanding the complexities of emotions, but it is a clever subterfuge for avoiding being honest with ourselves. For so many people the journey of discovery inside is the most forbidden and fear-filled territory ever, yet it is the key to successful lives and therefore essential for us as parents to make this journey and to share it with our children.

Instilling fear – calling it parenting

If we project our fear onto our child, as anger, we leave them confused and unsure, and they will internalise it against themselves because parents can't be that wrong, can they? Oh yes they can and often are. But parents change too and that is the best part. They can change and they can do it willingly and thoughtfully or their child will see them as very imperfect in later life, and will invariably have a difficult relationship with both parents and other adults around them, in work and personal life.

It is not wrong to release your anger. It is unskilful to project it onto someone else, especially if that person is a child. But being angry is yet another opportunity for you to learn with your child and explore with them after you have explored yourself, what happened and why it is not their responsibility.

Putting things right

You have made a mistake by being angry with your child, not for something that they have done but for revealing something that is deep and painfully buried within you. You have learned to recognise this and want to heal it. Acknowledge that:

- ◆ you have been wrong in the way that you responded
- ◆ you are going to learn your lesson from the experience
- ◆ it gives you an opportunity to explore what was the root cause of the reaction within yourself
- ◆ this is another opportunity for you to learn more about yourself and pass that learning on to your child.

Children of all ages, but especially over 7–8 years, can, in simple terms, understand many of the emotional growth choices that their parents are making. What better way to improve your child's self-esteem than to allow them the role of being your teacher? They can benefit from that in a positive way, so not only do we allow our children to learn their own lessons but we allow them to learn from us by observation rather than instruction. They can see the benefits to everyone for themselves so they also learn to think in this way. If children see that we make mistakes and are human, it has several positive effects:

- ◆ They love us anyway and they will love us in a whole sense which allows us to be wrong and to be human.
- ◆ It gives a positive meta-message, that it is OK to be wrong, even mum and dad do it.
- ◆ It allows them to openly forgive us and by openly forgiving them we actually heal the incidents as they occur.
- ◆ It prevents conflict building and continuing into adult life.
- ◆ It prevents points of conflict continuing within that relationship and filtering through into all adult relationships.

If this approach is adopted, it will become a simple and automatic form of interaction and fit naturally into family relationships.

A parent must exercise judgement in terms of explaining why they responded like that, what was the root cause of their response. This is not the same as using your child as unofficial counsellor and absolver. This is a very definite and important boundary.

- Work out your thoughts and feelings using a trained counsellor or trusted friend, away from your child.
- Then go to your child and say that you are very sorry that you hurt them in this way, it was your problem and not their responsibility.
- Never try and justify your actions, just state simply that it was a mistake and you are sorry.
- State what you should have done and that you will try to do that next time.

The biggest danger is using your learning and self-exploration as a way of justifying your behaviour. This is guilt and avoidance with the double bind of pretending honesty and openness. Justification is not needed if we are open to the learning and see where it comes from. We do not need to repeat our mistakes if we have learned from them. We only repeat our mistakes as parents when we are refusing to learn and will continue to do so until we have thought it through fully and learned all there is to know from it. Learning always occurs, whether we fight against it or remain open to it. One way is easier in the end, the open way.

Do:

- be honest and say, 'I did this and I was wrong'
- recognise there is no shame attached to being wrong.

Do not:

- make excuses for yourself by saying, 'I only did this because XYZ'
- say 'you don't like it when I do it, so that's how it feels like when you do it'.

Summary

When we consider discipline in relation to our children it is important to make sure it is a positive and constructive act.

- We all have only one responsibility in life, that is to live as truly to our inner selves as we can.
- As parents our sole responsibility to our children is to love them for their perfection and teach them to be true to themselves.
- We can only do this if we as parents also learn to live like this.
- If we do not, we teach our children to live with the same difficulties as ourselves, the same feelings of guilt, shame, fear, failure, etc.

CHAPTER 7

Creating Strong Boundaries

As already mentioned, having healthy boundaries is essential if we are going to realise our own potential or assist our child to do the same. They are the basis of the most productive approach to discipline and to guiding your child to make better choices for themselves.

Comparing boundaries and barriers

Boundaries and barriers are not at all the same, although they may appear so. The intention of both is to protect us. We will come back later to the question of what we need to be protected from. But it is the basis for each that is different.

- A healthy boundary is based on self-awareness and, consequently, self-esteem.
- It gives a quiet strength and absolute limit to our behaviour and to how we will allow ourself to be treated.
- A boundary is flexible and can be adapted to suit any changes, changes in direction that you make or in circumstances, or changes in our perception of things.
- If a boundary is challenged it does not cause us to struggle or feel threatened.

So boundaries are positive and helpful to have. Barriers are damaging and actually do the opposite.

- A barrier creates an illusion of safety and is based on fear. It keeps us separated from a part of ourself or our potential in order to avoid recognising the fear.
- A barrier is rigid. It doesn't let us change and it doesn't allow anything else out there to change. It just continues behaving in the same way, like a castle wall. Nothing can get past it, unless something happens to smash it, of course. We call that 'being hurt'.

- A barrier doesn't allow us to take a new look at experiences and move on from them. It asserts our right to stay as we are and for others to change.
- A barrier is an obstruction or an obstacle, preventing access or halting any movement, any advance. It is a hindrance, a restriction and an impediment.

Fear is the significant difference. There is no fear in a boundary, just self-knowledge and self-awareness, but there is a lot of fear in a barrier.

Absolute limits and flexibility

Boundaries are flexible as well as being absolute. They mark the maximum limit of what we will allow in any aspect of our life:

- the limits on what we will allow other people to do towards us and how much effect we will allow them in our life
- the limits on what we will choose to do or not to do regardless of pressure from others.

Boundaries find it easy to be flexible because they are based on our sense of trust in ourself, what we can adapt to, change and cope with. They're based on our ability to trust ourself to cope with a given situation and retain our own integrity. This is why they are so closely linked with self-esteem.

Boundaries and peer pressure

We can all be subject to peer pressure but children can be more vulnerable than adults. There are many choices we would prefer our children not to make for themselves, in the interests of their own safety. Obvious examples include taking drugs and generally putting themselves at risk. A barrier would have you saying, 'Oh no no no, I couldn't do that' and then you could be coerced or persuaded against your will. That is based on our fear of being wrong, or being rejected if we do not go along with the crowd.

So the barrier does not allow us freedom but a boundary does, it allows us to know our truth and to stick with it. It is based on that trust in ourself and our ability to make our own judgements. So we know that we do or do not want to do something.

Protecting or limiting

The more self-awareness and self-mastery we develop, the more we know that there is nothing to fear in life because nothing can hurt us if we do not allow it.

♦ Boundaries work on the basis of our strength of oneness with ourself.
♦ Barriers are based on our fear of separation from ourself.

When we know our own absolute truth, we can't be shifted from it. We can't be drawn back into negative, risk-taking behaviours or self-damaging behaviours. Nothing can touch us if we live in our own truth. That is our final ultimate protection because it knows there is nothing to protect from. So there is nothing to fear and we need no protection from anything when we have the truth because that does it all for us.

Developing healthy boundaries

We need to consciously consider our own parameters, and recognise that they are an intrinsic aspect of developing a continuing, healthy sense of self. They help us to make choices that are skilful, based on our self-respect and our respect for others.

A simple boundary might be that you would never lash out and hit anybody. This is your absolute limit on how you would allow yourself to behave. It is for both your own benefit and the benefit of other people.

> Some people don't know how far they can be pushed before a boundary gives, which means it is still in part a barrier, not a boundary, not an absolute.

A barrier can feel like a boundary because you feel convinced you'd never do it, and then something will happen when you would. A common example is 'I would never use violence unless I saw my child being attacked.' So then you have to reassess your boundary, how far you can be pushed. You may blame the experience for pushing you that far. That is an abdication of responsibility. Really it is showing you what you need to recognise inside yourself, that it is not a strong boundary, it is a barrier, based on a fear of violence.

Once you dissolve the fear you dissolve the barrier because you just know that you won't do that. You are safe because you have dealt with your fear of it and now have a solid boundary in place. You are not likely to face the situation because you do not carry it within your beliefs.

Many of us do have barriers rather than boundaries. The aim is to gradually change one into the other. We do this by exploring our thoughts and beliefs in depth. And as we do, so we can teach our children the same principles and beliefs for themselves. Our own boundaries will govern how we treat our children and teach them, by example, what to expect and do.

Case study: Jane _____

Jane was treated with some abuse and violence in her childhood, so she accepted violence as part of love – until she learned differently and said 'no'. Then when the pattern began to repeat with Keith she said 'no' more strongly. She was establishing her own boundaries about how people could or could not treat her and learning to say 'no'. _____

People with healthy boundaries:

♦ are very flexible and more able to respond to situations
♦ are very adaptable to change and go with the flow
♦ are very much less rejecting or critical of other people, regardless of their behaviour
♦ can differentiate between the person and their behaviour or choices
♦ are easier to get close to if you respect their boundaries
♦ tend to be more gentle or calm
♦ are less likely to get angry – they don't need to
♦ know what they will and won't do in life.

Feeling pushed

Most of the time everybody can find the limit to what they can cope with, and then find themselves pushed beyond it. That is how we find out and create and learn new ways of doing things.

- If we have a barrier demolished, we will feel fearful. There is little point in rebuilding it more strongly. It will continue to get knocked down, until we learn to do something different.
- A boundary will recognise its limit has been reached and reassess itself. We find new ways of developing those boundaries by experimenting with choices and learning from our own lessons.

Developing healthy boundaries is very much about taking responsibility back to yourself. Someone makes you behave in a way you don't like, it's not their fault, it's you. You did the behaviour, it's you, they didn't do it.

Boundaries are the parameters. They don't collapse if they are assaulted but they will show us vulnerabilities that we still need to work on.

Respecting your sense of self

Boundaries are based on a recognised choice of how to behave and what to allow in terms of other people's treatment of you, regardless of the provocation. If people behave inappropriately towards you and you allow it, that is a sign of your lack of respect for yourself. A sign of reclaiming that respect for yourself is to say:

- 'That is not appropriate behaviour.'
- 'I will not continue to allow that.'

Now you might find it possible to say that to yourself inside, but not to them in their face. You might become angry and aggressive towards them and feel justified in your response because 'they started it.' You still have choices. You can find some way of preventing them from continuing to treat you in that way. Choices include:

- not responding, engaging or being drawn
- responding in a different way
- walking away from the situation
- listening to their meta-message, recognising and accepting the basis of their fear.

A change in you will begin to break a pattern of behaviour based on power, control, abuse, or manipulative communication patterns. The key to dealing with abusive patterns is to recognise the truth in them and face it full on, like turning the light on to the shadows. That disarms their power. Keep going back to the truth if they are being manipulative or unkind, recognising their meta-message, until it has no power over you. Ultimately, however badly people are treating you, if they see it is not getting them anywhere, they will stop. One way or another they will stop, because the point of it is gone, which is to make themselves feel powerful and you feel powerless.

> Everyone's behaviour is a reflection of how they feel inside about themselves, not how they feel about others. Others simply reflect back things we cannot accept about ourself and wish to hide.

Developing boundaries in existing situations

It is never too late to change any situation or relationship. Boundaries require an assessment of the situation and behaviour involved, and a recognition of any agendas, including our agendas. If people are coming at us with certain kinds of behaviour and we are saying 'no', or if we are deciding to do things or not and where our parameters lie, we have got to recognise what our agendas are. Are there any games involved? Remember that everything in life is a mirror of all that we have inside us. Always and without any hesitation that is the case. For instance, are you giving in order to receive, or are you being given to in order that you will give back? Is that the deal? Is there a hidden trade-off between you and the other parties? Is it an open trade or is it manipulation? 'I'll do this favour for you and you do this favour for me.' If you're both open about what is going on there is no game, it's an open trade-off. That is a free choice between you.

If it is manipulation, not acknowledged, that means that one of you is doing something in order to get the other to do something else instead. And you're only doing something because you feel obliged, because of what they've done for you, not because you want to do that. That is going against your boundaries and your own truth. So, for instance:

- ◆ 'I let you do this because I want you to love me.'

or

- ◆ 'I let you do this because I love me and trust me and I love and trust you too.'

Compassion does not mean giving at your own expense, it means being compassionate to yourself, first and foremost, knowing that when you care for yourself you have more to give to others without being used or drained.

Boundaries and learning

Boundaries are flexible. The important thing is that they allow room for growth and movement. We need to recognise that we always, always, need to learn something else. We need to learn the next step in whatever lesson we're currently being faced with. We can only do our best all the time and keep moving.

Barriers repel love and laughter and any sense of joy at being alive. They're very stuck in victim attitudes, doom and gloom, can't trust anyone, beliefs. You *can* trust people, you've just got to be careful about whom you trust. But ultimately if you trust yourself you don't have to worry about trusting other people because you will be able to manage to deal with whatever they do anyway and with comfort. The issue is only ever coming back to yourself. So is your barrier based on a sense of shame of who you believe you are, or a fear of retribution, those sorts of things? Hopefully by now you have spent some time thinking about yourself, and you should know that there is nothing to be afraid of.

Learning to say 'no'

Boundaries are something that we learn and develop. They start in childhood where we are taught good boundaries or taught not to have boundaries, or we are taught to have barriers.

Boundaries are about saying 'no', either 'no, I won't do that' or 'no, you can't do that to me'. They're saying 'this is the limit'. They're saying 'yes, up to here and no further'. Where do you draw the line for yourself? Where do you say 'no'?

The difficulty in childhood is that we are often told that we cannot say 'no' to adults.

- If we're not allowed to say 'no' to parents or authority in childhood, at what point are we allowed to say 'no' to authority? When are we grown up?
- When do we get given permission: 'OK, now you're grown up you can say "no" to authority. You can now say "no, that is not acceptable". '?

We forget that we have any ability to say 'no' to anyone or anything at all that assumes authority over us. So we learn that we:

- can't say 'no'.

Instead we need to learn:

- who we can say 'no' to
- when we can say 'no'
- why to say 'no'
- when we can stop saying 'no'.

We learn that we can't say 'no' when we most need to. A little bit of bullying or aggression or some behaviour of power and that is where we allow ourselves to get damaged. That is where we need to think about boundaries for ourselves. But instead we create barriers to keep us safe and keep those others out. Instead we should have said 'that is not acceptable' right from the word go.

In existing relationships it can be very difficult to get back from that. But it is possible, if you are in that situation, to make better choices of response, to keep saying 'no'. They will eventually get the message. With children, you have to do this all the time.

Boundaries and privacy

Some children are never allowed to keep anything private from their parents. Early on in life this is not relevant but later on it is important for their sense of identity. Allowing children to have a sense of themselves and what they want to share means letting them establish what they want to be seen and what they want to keep private, to deal with independently or share with only a few special people. This includes:

- personal body privacy

- possessions
- achievements and struggles.

By allowing them to develop a sense of their own boundaries and privacy, children learn the difference between privacy and secrets. Secrets usually conceal abuse at all levels, including:

- shame and guilt
- sexual and physical abuse
- fear and bullying experiences
- beliefs in failure.

Boundaries and relationships

It is never too late to start establishing a boundary and letting the barrier down. In fact because you're letting down the barrier and creating a boundary, the other person feels safer, because you're letting them in. You're opening up to them in a way that will not put you at risk but in a way that will actually help to build a better relationship between both of you. You can keep reaffirming that boundary: 'No, this is not the way you treat me. Let's try it this way.'

Summary

A barrier is like wearing a corset, one of the old-fashioned ones, very tight and with a danger of the laces giving way. You are completely constricted and cannot move for fear of making the wrong move. You are held in and desperately hope that nothing gives way. A boundary is more like a comfortable jog top and pants, moving with you but still keeping you protected, not naked. You can move, dance, skip, lie down and generally let go in your life. It allows you to be your natural shape in life, to be who you really are.

- Boundaries find humour in the self and life generally.
- Barriers find humour in other people. If somebody else makes a mistake we laugh at them.
- A boundary will laugh with itself, because it is flexible and allows learning to occur, delighting in the process, allowing us to be wrong and to grow from it.
- A barrier wants to laugh at other people being wrong because

it doesn't want to be wrong itself. It is that relief that someone else is wrong, not me.

- ◆ A good boundary does not allow people to take advantage of you but allows you to have a good sense of humour and a good sense of your emotional response to any challenge as being honest, not full of fear, rejecting or defensive.
- ◆ Good boundaries stop you from behaving in ways that you will regret later on. But if you do they also allow you to learn and laugh from that as well.

CHAPTER 8

Understanding Love

T his chapter is a summary of much that has gone before, put into the context of our own and social expectations of the emotional bond between parent and child that we call 'love'. Most people assume that they love their child because he or she is their child, and that their child feels the same way about them. Although this is true to a degree, I want to break down the concept of love into several stages.

Defining love

We use the word 'love' and assume a common understanding and experience. Love is a concept and therefore nothing that we can physically see, hear, measure, touch, taste or smell. We understand it intuitively and this is where the differences come in. It is an experience of our emotions that can affect our physical sensations and our mental processes. It is a very powerful form of experience, yet it is one that is very misunderstood.

A concept as great as love is made up of many smaller ideas that are closely connected. For instance, if I say that 'I love rich chocolate ice cream', does that mean the same as 'I love my children'? Of course not and no one would really think of the use of the word in each context as actually meaning the same thing. In many ways it is more truthful to say 'I love rich chocolate ice cream' because we are unlikely to experience any fear in relation to ice cream whereas we can experience considerable fear in relation to our children. The greatest of these is surely fear of loss, which actually causes most parent/child separations at an emotional level. This is a simple example of how varied the ideas are behind the use of this term.

Misrepresenting fear as love

We learn about love from our experiences. If we experience love in the context of damaging, critical parenting, this is what love feels like for us. This is the same experience of love that has also filled us with low self-esteem and high self-doubt, and has held us back in our development. It is love subsumed by fear. So if love is the absence of fear, is this love? In other words, we call it love but it is not at all the real experience of love. Yet for many this is the closest they ever get.

Love for both self and another can be broken down to mean the following:

♦ accepting the other for whatever they are in reality
♦ recognising the inner core of pure love inside all of us
♦ respecting their right to make their own mistakes and learn their own lessons
♦ valuing positive qualities and accepting more complex ones
♦ recognising and valuing the lessons reflected back at us for our own benefit
♦ accepting that the other is doing the best they can with what they know
♦ respecting their right to make their own decisions in their own life
♦ offering supportive feedback when people have learned difficult lessons
♦ feeling and expressing warmth, concern and interest in the life and well-being of the other
♦ asking for, demanding and expecting nothing
♦ accepting the present as the only reality and rejecting fear of the past and future.

By now you should have worked through enough of the book to follow this section quite quickly. Simply enough, if you really want your child to grow and learn, give them the space to develop into healthy, emotionally stable and competent adults. This is the meaning of love. The common expectation placed on parents to control and discipline their children is contrary to the development of love and potential. All through this book I have referred to knowing your own truth. Trust and honesty is a vital part of love and respect. Teaching this to our children is not the problem – learning it for ourselves as parents is the main task.

Trust and honesty

I am looking at these two themes in terms of what they actually mean to us in our daily life.

- How do they affect us?
- Is there a single truth?
- Is it ever OK not to speak the truth?
- Is it ever OK to remain silent?
- What is the outcome of the choices we make in this area?

Trust is the basis for honesty and honesty is the basis for trust. You have to trust that people are honest with you and you have to be honest to be trustworthy. The most difficult thing for most people is saying what they really feel. In order to do that we must trust that it won't be used against us or dismissed in any way.

Being honest is difficult

Always telling the whole truth, all the time, is very very difficult for nearly all of us – almost to the point where we are not sure any more what the truth is. As children we all start out by speaking the truth, but we are told off or punished for it. We are told that we are tactless, or rude, or unkind. Our truth has been dismissed, or laughed at. Or it has been blatantly denied because the adults around us, for whatever reason and often quite unconsciously, didn't want to hear what we were saying. They wanted to stop us saying it, so they could pretend it wasn't there. They couldn't cope with the honesty of what we were expressing. That was their fear and shame and guilt, not ours, but it silenced us anyway. So we have difficulty in maintaining any trust and honesty that we were born with.

Learning about honesty

Children all start by speaking and expressing their truth, but this is denied and they learn to express something else. However, as there are no negative experiences only learning opportunities, having lived with what life is like not telling the truth, we can know how much better the truth is once we recognise and return to it. So these experiences teach us the value of trusting and being trusted, of being honest and being treated honestly in return.

Most of all we learn how much better it is when you can get back to honesty again, but with the wisdom of an adult and an understanding of the effects of a lack of honesty.

Adapted truth, adapted self

Often we tend to portray a self that is more an adapted self, a term which comes from transactional analysis. We become what we think others want us to be and not our true self. This is a damaged or distorted version of our self and it doesn't actually do us any good to do that because it twists us inside. The more we become the adapted self, the more we damage the true self because we are also denying the right of the true self to exist.

Honesty is of paramount importance to ourselves. I'm not suggesting that you suddenly start telling blunt truths all over the place. It does need to be skilfully handled but it is crucial because ultimately we can't trust anybody if we don't know that they are totally honest with us.

> We all need someone to be genuine with us and for us to be genuine and honest with.

Hiding from truth

We hide from the painful experience of those adults' responses to our early attempts to express the truth, yet that is what we most need in order to get back to that level of clarity and honesty but with the wisdom of an adult. You need total honesty in a close relationship to get the best out of it. Most of us, however, settle for an overall general honesty and accept that there will be areas of dishonesty.

- This closes down areas of the relationship.
- Certain areas of us are also closed down in the process.

And that is what it really comes back to – we close down a part of ourself by allowing dishonesty to occur within a relationship. This prevents a fully sharing, supportive, feedback relationship developing, one that is open and loving. What we are saying is that we need to hide a part of ourself because it is not acceptable, or we fear that if that part of ourself is shown then someone will reject us. That is a denial of self. Any need to hide a part of yourself is a lack of trust that that self is acceptable in some way. Ultimately there is nothing unacceptable in any of us because we are all doing the best we can with what we know.

The truth about us

There is no such thing as a negative characteristic, only good characteristics being used in the wrong place or in the wrong way. We have not yet learned how to utilise and manage that aspect of our self properly. There is nothing fundamentally wrong with any of us and if we could be totally honest and open about who we are to everybody, and everyone was the same, we would not have half the difficulties we have.

It is the idea that we have to hide certain bits and feel ashamed of them that is harmful, and because everyone is doing it to everyone else it feels as if this is normal and safe. Other people are so quick to judge and say, 'Ha ha, I found you out', hoping that they cannot be found out themselves. These are power games and distortions and they are what cause the difficulties in expressing the truth.

We accept that fear as our own and are silenced by it. Although it is going on all around us, it is up to us, for our own benefit, to decide not to collude with that and not to do it to ourselves. Not to play any dishonest games and say, 'OK, I'm going to walk my truth and speak my truth and live my truth.' If we live with our truth then we and others can always trust us. Even if it's not always nice, they feel secure in our integrity.

Honesty and games

You cannot say to someone what you really feel if you do not trust that:

◆ your honesty will be respected and treated with dignity
◆ it will not be used against you at a later date
◆ it will not be diminished or used as a way of patronising you
◆ it will not be ignored or dismissed as unimportant.

Until you have learned to trust that your real self is acceptable and that others will therefore accept it, the tendency is to portray

yourself as someone other than your real self, to hide your
thoughts or feelings. Often we then also hide them from ourselves,
so that:

- we no longer know what we are really thinking and feeling and
  live in an emotional fog
- we try to become what we think others want us to be, not who
  we really are
- we adopt roles and scripts which support this created self and
  wonder why it never quite feels as good as it ought to, why
  every so often something seems to erupt from within and push
  its way to the surface, betraying our mask
- we become an adapted version of ourselves and wonder why it
  feels awkward even though we become convinced that this is
  who we really are.

Honesty with ourself

Truth is of paramount importance because by hiding our truth we
damage ourselves, both emotionally and physically. If we cannot
trust ourselves to be completely honest with ourselves, and with
others, how can we begin to trust other people? Yet trust is the
fundamental basis of all healthy emotional relationships. It is the
crucial lesson learned in the first year of life, according to Eric
Erikson a follower of Freud.

Truth and conscience

Our conscience always knows if we have been dishonest and it
builds up inside us, just as we always know when we have been
told a lie and it is a truth we know inside us. We cannot hide from
that which we know deep inside our consciousness. No matter
how well we justify the untruth we have spoken, it is still an
untruth.

Telling the truth at all times is the challenge and we should start
by telling ourselves the truth. This means taking responsibility for
all that we do and say and not finding justifications and excuses
for our behaviour. It means not blaming others or external factors
for making us do things we would rather not have done, or we
would rather not remember, or not have others know about. It

means not blaming the past for things we are doing right here in the present. It means looking for the hidden fears which we are holding on to and which we need to release. Finding the truth often means digging deeply.

Being nice

The truth is not always pretty or nice, it is not always easy or comfortable, but it is the truth. It is not always polite, although that is more to do with manner of expression rather than content or intention. Sometimes it is very uncomfortable both to say and to hear, but it is the truth, and as such it cannot be wrong.

- ◆ You can be nice and be lying.
- ◆ You can be comfortable and be lying.

Bending the truth twists our emotions, and causes us distress and damage. If you are the one wanting to be nice and not telling the truth to do this, you are twisting yourself inside. Your conscience knows that it was not the truth and knows why you did not tell the truth or act honestly.

You might think it does not matter in the short term, but in the long term we collect these emotional blockages until they make us unable to tell the truth at all. We lose our ability to trust ourself, and if we cannot trust ourself we cannot trust others. Telling anything other than the truth at all times undermines love at all levels and totally blocks a full realisation of our potential.

Truth and hurt

If we do not tell the truth we hurt ourselves but we also hurt others, even if they do not want to hear the truth and may even try to stop us expressing ourselves. Do we want to hurt those we love the most?

> Usually we justify telling an untruth by saying it's so as not to hurt others. Stop for a moment right now and think – what would you rather have, the truth or a sugar-coated lie?

Does it not feel patronising to think that the people around you consider that you cannot cope with the truth and so they tell you an untruth or a variation of the truth or a half-truth instead? Children especially need to know the truth, or how are they:

- to learn to make good choices in life
- to know themselves and accept both themselves and others
- most importantly, to trust?

Truth and feedback

When we tell people half-truths or untruths, we deny them the right to have honest feedback about themselves, which they need in order to understand themselves and move on from a difficult situation in their own lives. We deny them what they need to assess, to learn and grow in themselves. We betray their trust in our honesty. Feedback is not criticism or judgement, it is saying:

- you are OK
- but that is not an appropriate way to behave.

If we remain silent, the other person does not have a chance to adjust their behaviour. Giving truthful feedback means giving them the chance to put things right. By saying, 'I have a bit of a problem with that XYZ', we give them the opportunity to change. We are not saying 'you are wrong', we are saying 'I have the problem'. People don't do things to annoy us, we choose to be annoyed – they might like to know how to help us.

As for ourselves, we damage our conscience, because even if no one else ever knows we did not tell the truth, we do. However hard we try to justify it, we know we did not speak in complete and open honesty and we cannot ever hide from that, we can only suppress it or admit it and release and forgive ourselves. If we do not, then we will need to expend a great deal of additional energy in keeping this knowledge suppressed and often tell further untruths to protect the first one, so it becomes an avalanche that wants to sweep us away or a burden we cannot manage.

> The truth is not subjective, as Nietzsche would have had us believe. A subjective truth is a truth that we have created in our own minds to make it more comfortable for us to live with.

Subjective truths are also untruths, even though some people become so good at telling themselves these lies that they believe they are the truth. But they are not and being angry with people who expose these inconsistencies is not the answer, especially if this is your child showing you an image of yourself that you do not like. The answer is to look at yourself and see other people as a mirror showing you something of great value and importance about yourself. They are offering you the chance to change and heal. There is no point in trying to convince them or yourself that they are wrong and your version of the truth is right. It will not make it so, it will only take energy to suppress this untruth further and leave you unhappy inside.

Truth and guilt

If you tell a truth and someone rejects it, remember, this is not your responsibility, it is theirs. They have chosen to respond in this way. It is their fear of the truth and their problem, not yours. Making people feel guilty for telling the truth is a common form of manipulation, a good way of silencing people and keeping the illusion of the distorted truth alive. Similarly if you are made to feel guilty for not saying something that you do not want to say, which is not your truth, that is a manipulation of your truth against you and you should recognise it and remain true to yourself.

Using fear to control or conceal the truth is an untruth in itself. Often the fear is of rejection, 'If I tell this truth I will be rejected, so I will tell something else', or it is fear of many other controlling behaviours like sulking, derision, silence, withdrawal and outbursts of anger. Whatever mechanism is being used to keep you from speaking your truth, it is up to you to overcome it. It is your challenge.

Truth and tact

Tactfulness is a common form of untruth – saying something so as not to hurt someone's feelings. Most people feel uneasy or are too scared to face the truth and accept tact as an acceptable justification for untruth. They may accept our reassurance on the surface but at some level they do know the truth. Otherwise they

would not have asked for our comments or taken any notice.
Don't be nice and protect someone's feelings. It is deeply
patronising. Loving feedback means telling them something in
order to help them, not to judge or criticise. It is not about
'putting them down' but about how their behaviour affects you.

Often, coupled with tact, we say something to the other's face
and something different behind their back. This is not the truth.
Whom are you trying to protect? Yourself? From the truth about
your unkind attitudes, from the idea that you might not be nice?
How nice is it to tell untruths and conceal truths?

Silence is as big an untruth as saying an untruth. it is still a
concealment of the truth and a denial of feedback, a withholding
of information which is patronising and unkind.

Finally learning to be honest and trust yourself is one of the
best gifts you can give yourself and it will last you a lifetime.
Although it may seem hard to learn at first, like riding a bicycle,
you will find it becomes much easier in time. Don't give up on
yourself. Never think 'this is too hard' just do it in small steps, first
with yourself, and then gradually taking it out to your whole
emotional environment. Ultimately the truth is your protector, it
protects you from the damage that untruth will do and it allows
you to remain true to yourself. Ultimately it is up to us to make
that commitment to ourselves, to live our whole truth with
respect for self and others, and everyone else can do what they
like. If they do not like our truth that is their problem not ours.
Do not be silenced from your truth in order to please others. If we
live our truth, nothing can really hurt us.

Letting go and allowing your child to learn

Most parents find that letting go is the hardest aspect of love.
Indeed it is hard for all of us and adults who have experienced
broken relationships will recognise just how hard and sometimes
how long it takes to let go of a relationship which has come to the
end of its useful life and has been unable to evolve into a new
framework. This however, is what we need to do, and this is in fact
what we are doing in small stages from the moment a child is
born.

- We physically let go and allow them to sleep alone as a baby. The baby learns the lessons of togetherness and separateness on a physical level. We are here when they wake to care for them, so they learn separation and trust.
- Once your child has mastered the skill of balance and can walk, you no longer watch them as carefully. You let them make mistakes, i.e. falling over, bumping into things, etc., so that they can perfect the technique.

This is easy and expected but the further up the levels we get, the harder it becomes. Letting go:

- allows parents to recognise how much their child can achieve without their help and intervention
- recognises that you are giving yourself a vote of confidence in your own parenting skills
- demonstrates your trust that your guidance has equipped them to learn their lessons and make sensible decisions
- shows your trust and respect for them and your belief that they will exercise their learning and discover new lessons.

This is the same level of love that we demonstrate when we support them with their learning. This should be done without recourse to fear, guilt, shame or anger for parent or child. Ask them questions and let them draw their own conclusions. Let them find their own learning.

Helping your child to confront fear

Most of the time we are unable to act as we might because we are afraid of outcomes and the responsibility that gives us. It is the burden of responsibility layered up with fears such as guilt which turn a simple decision into a major trauma and may leave us unable to act at all. We remain passive and let things happen to us.

This is not the road to success, it is simply a responsibility-minimising strategy for dealing with life. It is a high-risk approach because you may not get the outcome you could have had if you had taken a pro-active role in the decision-making. The only let-out clause is that you didn't overtly do anything, so you can disclaim responsibility. It is important to remember that inactivity is still a decision. Avoidance is a choice:

- not to participate in the full potential of life
- not to take risks and test out your skilfulness
- not to learn, change and develop towards a full realisation of your potential.

Fear-based avoidance of decision-making is common in people who have not been allowed to make risky decisions for themselves in childhood, or for whom the risks that went wrong were heavily laden with negative responses from parents.

Children and adults need low criticism and high praise for potential to be realised. Mistakes should not be hushed up and should not attract criticism. They should be quietly accepted as part of the perfect human being achieving their own perfection through their own lessons. The hardest times for parents are when:

- children behave in ways which attract disapproval from others, e.g. family, other parents and teachers
- children want to extend their sense of freedom and independence before the parent feels ready to let them (but says the child is not ready)
- children learn some hard lessons, like Sam or Megan (see pages 61 and 74)
- children reject something, someone, an interest or viewpoint that is valued by a parent
- children confront parents with their own worst fears.

Try it now   This is a simple exercise which should be useful to follow and adapt to any of the above situations as they arise. Take time to reflect on each of the questions in turn and make a note of your answers.

- What response options do you have?
- What is the most positive outcome of each option?
- How important will the best possible outcome be in five years/six weeks?
- What is the worst that could happen from each option?
- How important will the worst possible outcome be in five years/six weeks?
- How great is the risk of things going badly?
- What is the outcome you want?

This exercise is a mental letting go of fear through rational positive thinking. It releases the tendency to react with fear, through either anger or controlling decisions, and allows the parent to discuss their concerns with the child. And then allow the child to decide or negotiate and therefore learn to take responsibility for their actions. This will include making mistakes and learning hard lessons, but it will lead to an adult who is able to make decisions and accept the responsibility for their own lives. It will make them able to act without the restrictions of fear and achieve their potential.

Letting go of fear for parents

A child who has learned how to make decisions for themselves within safe boundaries, provided for them by society and family life, is able to participate fully as they enter adult life. In order to do this the parent must learn to let go and allow the child to learn his or her lessons. One of the hardest things a parent has to do is to sit back and watch a child making a mistake. The desire to intervene and protect is very great. But as we have seen, protecting children can leave them unable to cope later as adults and will undermine their self-esteem and independence. If parents hold on to the decision-making for their children they will feel less fear in the short term, but in the long term they are unable to trust their child when he or she is out of control/sight. A child who is very restricted at home will usually act in one of three ways when freed from the constraints:

- They will be unable to make decisions for themselves and will not participate in life.
- They will want to participate in life but will be easily led by an influential member of a peer group.
- They will want to make their own decisions and will rush around making them without knowing what they are doing or why.

All these are high-risk behaviours for anyone and are common in many young adults and adolescents. It is the result of a society that still talks in terms of controlling children rather than nurturing them. Children who do not have clear personal boundaries, but have developed barriers as a form of self-protection, are more likely to desire to conform to a group identity rather than stand alone.

Thinking for oneself

Research into group conformity clearly showed the importance of knowledge, and that confidence in one's own decision is crucial for withstanding pressure from a group to agree with something against one's better instincts. Crutchfield (1955) showed that people who are more likely to conform with a group, even if they do not believe in the group position, have:

+ poorer social relationships
+ less leadership ability
+ less self-sufficiency
+ less ego strength
+ feelings of inferiority
+ a narrow-minded and inhibited outlook
+ more submissive tendencies
+ low self-awareness and insight into own emotions.

One of the hardest letting-go times in a parent's life is during adolescence, when we have to let them go out in the evenings and often do not know where they will end up. This is the time when we worry about whether they will end up taking drugs, getting into fights, drinking and taking risks with sexual behaviour, to list but a few parental nightmares. If we have allowed our child to make decisions throughout their childhood, then they will now use these skills to their best advantage and only do what they themselves feel safe doing. Group pressure will not lead them into taking undue risks which could have long-term consequences. Even if they do start to try these areas of adolescence out for themselves, they will very quickly weigh up the pros and cons for themselves and make their own decisions based on a knowledge of why they have made that decision for themselves.

Further research (Willis, 1963) shows three types of conformity and non-conformity:

+ those who move towards the majority group norms and adhere to them

- those who move towards anti-majority group norms and oppose the majority but still adhere to a minority group norm
- those who have a lack of consistency in moving towards or away from a group norm and remain independent of groups generally.

Children are not born into one of these groups, they are socialised into them. Only people of the third type are free from the group rule and therefore more likely to make their own decisions and stick to them. These are the people who have learned their lessons and are comfortable with themselves. These are successful people.

Trusting your child

So you have finally allowed yourself to sit back and let go. Your child is now making their own decisions and learning the skills that will enable them to mature into balanced adults. You are letting them make their own mistakes and showing confidence in their ability to make decisions and accept responsibility for the consequences of their actions. They will still make mistakes and those mistakes may have quite serious consequences, but they are still young and will learn fast at this stage if they are allowed to. This is the greatest sign of respect that you can give your child. The meta-message of trust and respect for their ability to deal with errors of judgement will have several effects:

- They will be comfortable with their achievements.
- They will remain open to learning from their mistakes.
- Their self-esteem and self-confidence will continue to grow.
- They will become more self-reliant.

Summary

Love is a concept made up of many component parts, including trust, honesty, letting go and challenging all aspects of fear. By doing this for ourselves we do the same for our child and teach them to do it for themself.

- Trusting yourself and your child to learn and grow from life experiences is the greatest way of demonstrating love.
- It involves not being afraid of the truth, not wanting to be

nice, but having the courage to use tough love and feedback.

- It means recognising that the individual who can make their own judgements and decisions, and who can accept responsibility, can only do this through their sense of acceptance of all that they do, think, feel and say.

CHAPTER 9

Stories allow us to explore ideas, thoughts and feelings from a safe distance.

Using Stories as Metaphors

T he tradition of storytelling has been present throughout history and lives within all cultures. Scheherezade kept herself alive by telling stories that were sufficiently compelling to keep her audience and would-be executioner interested. Within Arab culture, storytelling was recognised as a way of earning a living – the better you were at telling your stories to the audience in the market, the more successful you were. Other cultures have special times, such as marriage or transitional life stages, set aside for telling stories, or stories for specific times of the year, such as after the harvest. Storytelling has a long tradition of verbal performance. The stories were seen as rich treasure which would be taught, as well as the correct way to tell them, although each storyteller would develop their own interpretation, so that stories would evolve over time.

In our culture it is very much the tradition to share stories with young children at bedtime, usually in order to calm a child and give them something imaginative and fun to think about before they sleep. The choice of story is quite important as anything which arouses strong emotions will have an opposite effect to helping the child sleep.

Storytelling is also a tradition in nursery and primary schools. Because this is during the day, it is possible to use material which is more challenging. Some children enjoy stories which contain quite extreme violence, like the story of The Fox and the Blue Grapes (see Chapter 11). The safety of a fictional setting allows exploration of these feelings without actually putting anyone at risk.

Developing imagination

The imagination is both a versatile tool and a rich resource for humans to work with. From the imagination comes all creative and original thought. Without it we would never have evolved as a species. Yet this incredible gift that we have is dismissed as 'just your imagination', i.e. not real. How real is a thought? It is a thought that initiates all advance, all inventions, all progress, all learning and knowledge, all scientific and medical progress. Thought creates reality in a material sense just as much as in a perceptual sense. Our creative thinking patterns are the richest resource we have and the most innovative thoughts come from the imagination. Imagination works from the unconscious mind and from the right side of the brain, the creative side.

By using stories, imagery and metaphor, it is possible:

◆ to access the learning patterns laid down within the banks of previous experience
◆ to develop new learning patterns for specific purposes.

Most learning is held subconsciously and we remain unaware of how and why we feel certain things. Yet these experiences affect our immediate behaviour and our perception of new experiences. Neuro Linguistic Programming (NLP) and other psychological techniques use this potential of the brain to retrain the mind and create new structures of reality. It is possible to explore old belief systems and challenge them, to change to a new way of thinking. We can do this for ourselves as parents as well as helping our children to develop alternative models of reality that are not based on fear and limitation.

Two levels of mind

Stories work with both the conscious and unconscious mind. We relate on both levels, are stimulated on both levels, conjure up a visual representation from the words, relate to the emotions and behaviour of characters within the stories. Stories are also a rich resource for art, with many representations of stories like George and the Dragon, Venus and Mars, Adam and Eve, the Trojan Horse, to name but a few.

In order to maximise this connection and enhance the learning from each story, there are a range of practical activities you can carry out with your child. Select one that will interest your child the most and maximise their abilities, rather than choosing one that you might think most suitable. These stories must be explored by the child in the way that is most attractive for them if any incidental learning is to occur.

Activities

1 Draw themselves in a similar way to one of the characters in one of the stories.
2 Draw pictures to go with each story or model characters from clay or make a collage or wall frieze.
3 Turn one of the stories into a cartoon picture strip with speech balloons.
4 Write a poem based on one of the stories.
5 Write a speech by one of the characters explaining how they felt about what happened.
6 Write a story about themselves in a way that is similar to one of the stories. For example, using the holly tree story, think about a time when they felt different, outside, unnoticed, alone, with low self-esteem.
7 Rewrite the story with a different ending.
8 Rewrite the story from the point of view of a different character, e.g. the fox, or Violet's parents.
9 Make a list of things that they like about themselves. Really help them to develop this list.
10 Make a list of all the things that they don't like about themselves. Really help them to develop this list as well.
11 Discuss each of the items on the 'negative' list and discuss ways of showing that these things might also be good in a different situation.

Using empathy

If we enjoy a story we will have become involved. We will have thought, felt and allowed the story to become part of us, our whole experience, for the amount of time it has taken to listen to it. Like emotions, stories have energy and also contain symbolism, which is why they are healers. This energy is like electricity in many ways: a story can enlighten you, animate you, motivate you, extend you and offer your endless possibilities. You cannot see the energy, only the result of it. Stories told at the wrong time and in the wrong way can have little or no desired effect at all. Coercing a child to listen to a story will have little benefit. It is the willingness and enjoyment that enhances the learning and enables a child to be relaxed and open to the learning contained within the story. Children who have had very difficult lives are encouraged by therapists and care workers to make stories of their own lives as a way of finding their own identity and healing their own lives.

Diffusing fear

Stories allow us as parents to discuss difficult and sometimes painful issues with our child from a safe distance. It is the position of security that allows us to remain confident and open to the learning. Making a child feel fear in advance of a situation will make it harder for them to cope if the reality occurs, and will make it more likely to occur.

- How else can you prepare a child for the possibility of bullying at school or help them cope with domestic violence?
- How can a child explain their lack of confidence or self-esteem before they understand the concepts behind it and the language to use?

Life will never be perfect and indeed I hope that this book has demonstrated the importance of facing and dealing with difficulty as an essential part of emotional development. There will always be other people who are hurt or damaged in their experience of life and these are the people we have to learn to cope with. They have to learn to cope with their own lives. The only responsibility anyone has is to themselves and to their children, to teach them how to be responsible for themselves.

Many themes in one story

The stories beginning on page 135 are designed to be flexible in the range of issues they explore. By talking about the experiences of a fictional character, a child is able to identify their thoughts and feelings through empathy with the experiences of the character in the story. This is a basis for storytelling throughout history and across cultures. It is the basis of the excellent book by Estes called *Women who Run with Wolves*, which looks at all the original folk stories and the commonality of themes across cultures. I have adapted The Sour Grapes fable by Aesop, written one original story called Violet, based on folklore and the concept of myths having purpose, and taken a traditional theme for The Holly Tree.

Using the child's natural empathy with the characters in the book, a parent can prepare and discuss issues that have already arisen or might arise. Certainly the more prepared a child is before an event, the more they will be able to cope with it and not be taken by surprise.

Sharing stories with your child can be the safest situation from which to learn about life's nasty surprises. It is the security and intimacy of this setting which allows informal and very effective learning to take place. It is possible to discuss the issues in a story as it is followed through, stopping and discussing aspects, or reading the story through and then using it as a basis for discussion of life experiences.

Accessing the unconscious mind

The unconscious mind is easily accessed through the right side of the brain because it does not engage the logical, conscious, left-brain thought-processes.

In dreams we are presented with a range of stories in which we are involved, and often also those around us from everyday life. The content of dreams is often recalled as disjointed and quite impossible in our conscious sense of reality, but in the dream it happened. Up until a century or so ago people would dream of flying and think it quite ridiculous, yet flying is now seen as a normal method of travel.

What is dreaming?

Much work has been done on the importance of dreaming, how long and how often it occurs. It is usually reckoned to occur during REM (rapid eye movement) sleep (Schachter and Singer) and there is evidence that some people experience lucid dreaming, i.e. dreams that the dreamer is controlling (Hearne). However, we are still unsure as to why we do dream. Jung and Freud both believed that dreams are the best and most accurate access to understanding the unconscious mind. Dreams are seen as a way of working out emotional conflicts and living fantasies in safety. Part of the story of Violet and all The Fox and the Blue Grapes came from a dream I had.

Stories and perspectives

Stories allow us to think about experiences from a different perspective. We can reframe the experiences of a child from negative to positive by using a story which shows how outcomes can be unexpected and difficulties often turn out to be the best thing that could have happened. The child might be part way through a difficult time in their lives, or still experiencing the difficulty even if it has ended in actuality, but because of the negative emotions connected to the experience, they are blocked from gaining any benefit. Stories can be used to extend and open up these possible futures for a child and help them to see that all is not lost. Good things come round too and if we are too busy feeling sorry for ourselves we might just miss the opportunity.

Healing ideas through stories

Many experiences can be too painful for us to cope with at a conscious level and in a direct way, but stories can penetrate the defence mechanisms in a safe and indirect way, thus allowing changes to occur. This is a powerful form of emotional healing that is used by therapists and in many forms. It is also the basis of other art therapies. Jung believed that creativity is essential for mental health.

Stories are healing because we become disconnected from ourselves for a short period of time. For the duration of the story we can forget our own limitations and become anything we choose, identifying with characters in the story. Children often like toys which they associate with stories from books or TV characters, and will play games which extend this fantasy of endless possibilities in a completely safe way. In the same way, many adults like to read escapist books and see high adventure fast action films in a way that is safe.

The more you put yourself into the story the more medicine you receive – the more learning, the more healing and the more understanding you get. It is very much a question of what you give out, you get back. There are no mistakes in life, only lessons to be learned. The more prepared for the exam we are, the better. Real experience is the exam, stories are the swotting. The more swotting we do, the better the outcome. Let us not slip into the idea that we can wing it on the day because maybe we will and maybe we won't but it will be much harder that way. Swotting for life using stories is really not as hard as swotting for school exams and if you and your child share the experience, the learning will be wonderful.

The language of stories and poems is very often similar to the experiences we have in dreams, but in a more cohesive form. A story can go anywhere and take any form. It is not real but it can represent real life and it can feel real. Dream analysis has been understood for centuries and across healing perspectives as central to understanding the mind and the influence of mind over body. Dreams occur in an unconscious state and the interpretation is done at a conscious level. Stories are experienced at a conscious level and penetrate the subconscious.

Teaching throughout history

Storytelling as a means of teaching about life has many very significant models of excellence. All the major religions use stories to illustrate a point. The Bible is a rich source of stories which can be told for their own interest, and enable us to consider ideas and situations in a non-religious way if we choose. All the great philosophers used stories as a way of explaining the growth and development of the individual through adversity. Many of the myths of Greece, Rome, Egypt and other ancient cultures are evidence of this.

Try it now

Think back to stories you read as a child.

- How did they affect you and influence you?
- Were they treated as stories and therefore not to be taken seriously?
- How many of them do you still remember in a special way?

Unfortunately too often western society dismisses creative thought as not being logical and yet it is only creative thought that brings about changes and sees alternative solutions to problems. It is through creative thought that we can really explore the full creativity of our humanity.

___

Stories and skills

Historically stories were used to teach about life, but in modern western culture there seems to be too much emphasis on using stories as 'an enjoyable way of learning to read'. In other words, the story is only a means to acquiring skills needed in adult life and this is its primary function. It is not seen as a special and useful tool in its own right.

This is missing the whole point about stories. It is detrimental to the lives of many children and adults because it is depriving them of the real value of stories, which is to learn about life in safety. The tradition of the spoken story is mostly lost. Very few people go out for an evening to listen to someone telling stories. Yet this was the tradition in inns and on street corners in previous centuries. Performance poetry is still a minority interest, supported only by other poets in the main. The advent of cheaper publishing techniques has made books more accessible. Films and TV are other ways of experiencing stories, but none are as rewarding as having a story read to you. The nearest we get to that is in childhood when we are learning to read, and the pleasure of reading can be destroyed as part of this process. Children with dyslexia find it hard to read for themselves, but because they often have better visual imagery skills, can memorise the story from hearing it and enjoy a far richer, internal imagery, of the story content.

The gift of a story

Stories are like gifts from the teller to the listener.

- It is a giving of your time and all your concentration in the telling of the story.
- It is a gift of your skills in making different tone and volume, in giving voices to the characters in the story, of placing emphasis and emotion into the story.

This has valuable meta-messages for a child. It is telling them that they are worth your effort.

Developing reading skills

It is always a good idea to prepare yourself for reading the story and know it in advance. Then you can concentrate on using your voice to bring it to life. There is a significant difference in the reading by someone who has read a story through a couple of times themselves and has prepared themselves to become involved with the telling. If you read the stories first before you talk to your children you can also read the suggested interpretations of each story so that you can explore the issues more fully during the telling. You can also find a greater range of possible uses for each story. The stories beginning on page 135 have both suggested interpretations and activities for following up with. You may find that you will also see the stories in a newer and deeper light. You may find yourself thinking and learning from them too. Stories are not just for children, they are for everyone. Adults can gain as much from a child's story and even more since they will identify the ironies and subtleties more clearly.

Stories that are written as metaphors can be revisited because they mean something different each time. Life will have continued throwing you opportunities for learning and your perception will continue to grow. The Fox and the Blue Grapes might resonate with bullying one week and with feeling insecure and unable to communicate the next.

Children can rewrite the story in their own words. This is a good way of recognising how they have interpreted the story and what they have identified with in it. There are follow-up activities which they can do which extend the depth to which the child has empathised with the characters and experiences in the story.

Summary

Stories are the richest source of learning that we can use apart from real life itself. They stimulate thoughts and feelings that may remain buried in the unconscious. Just because something is buried in the unconscious does not mean it is healed. In fact it means the very opposite. The hurt is deep and still there, creating limitation in our lives and reducing our potential.

- ◆ Stories allow us to consider possibilities in life without needing to create anxiety about 'what might happen to me'.
- ◆ Imagination and creative thinking processes allow us to

reprogramme our own limitation beliefs.
- Stories illustrate the difference between skilful and less skilful choices in a given situation. They show the consequences and allow us to recognise the value of those choices.
- Stories create a bond of intimacy between the people sharing them, between the parent and the child, allowing a shared experience for discussion.

The Stories

CHAPTER 10

The Little Holly Tree

A long time ago, deep in the middle of a very old forest, there grew a young holly tree. She grew tall and strong, growing up towards the sky, until she was nearly as big as some of the other trees around. For many years the holly tree put so much energy into growing that she didn't notice all the other trees in the forest.

Then one day the little holly tree stretched out her long branches, shook her prickly dark green leaves and looked around.

Standing right next to the holly tree was a tall chestnut tree. His branches and twigs were covered with buds but they were all sticky and brown. 'How strange,' thought the holly tree, looking at her own tiny green ones, 'I wonder why the chestnut tree is so different?' The holly tree shook her branches and rustled her leaves a little more to wake up the sleepy old chestnut tree, but he stood dozing in the spring sunshine.

Suddenly the forest started to fill with lots of different noises. Squeaks and shouts and stomps and thumps. The holly tree didn't know what these noises meant so she looked around eagerly to see what was happening. She felt quite excited at all the new things that she was seeing for the first time.

At that moment lots of children came running through the trees. They came running up to the chestnut tree and danced round him, all holding hands and singing and calling out to each other. Then they stopped dancing and started to pick some of the twigs with the big brown buds on. As they did so the holly tree could hear them talking: 'How nice the twigs will look when the leaves start to open. We can put them in pots of water and stand them on the windowsills.'

The holly tree was fascinated and waited for the children to turn around and take some of her buds home too. She rustled her leaves proudly and shook her branches, but the children didn't take any of the holly tree's twigs at all. None of the children seemed even to notice the holly tree, no matter how hard she tried to shake her branches and rustle her leaves. When the children had gone, she felt sad, and for a few days stopped looking around. The forest suddenly seemed too quiet and lonely. But she was too curious to know about everything and so soon she started to look around again.

Nearby was a hawthorn tree close to the edge of the wood. The hawthorn tree was looking very pretty, covered in snowy white blossom and fresh light green leaves with pretty edges.

'How pretty you are,' thought the holly tree, looking at her own plain green leaves with sharp prickles all around the edges. She looked at her flowers, too, but they were so small that you could hardly tell they were there. And she felt a little sad again.

Then she heard the noises of singing and dancing again and cheered up very quickly. 'Maybe the children have come to see me this time,' she thought. The children came running and dancing into the forest. They were carrying all sorts of bags and blankets. They ran right past the holly tree and right up to the hawthorn tree. They joined hands and danced round her, just as they had danced round the chestnut tree. The little holly tree looked on, still hoping that they would visit her this time. But the children stopped their dances and collected some of the may blossom. They clipped it into their hair and danced round the hawthorn tree all over again, laughing and clapping with joy. Then the oldest children took out a big rug and spread it out under the boughs of the hawthorn tree. They all sat down on it to eat their picnic.

The holly tree watched the children and thought how nice it would be if they came to dance round her when they had finished eating. But when they had finished their picnic, they all danced round the hawthorn tree once more, then went home. The holly tree didn't like her dark prickly leaves any more. She wanted soft light green leaves like the other trees and big white blossoms. She dropped her branches a little and decided not to look around so much.

A few weeks later the holly tree heard the sound of the children coming back into the forest again. She didn't look up to begin with. But soon her curiosity got the better of her and she wondered if they might come and see her this time. Still the children didn't come near to the holly tree. This time they went to the old beech tree that stood in the centre of the forest. His big branches were low to the ground and spread out wide across the forest floor. The children climbed into the beech tree. Some climbed up a little way and some climbed right up to the top of the tree. They used the patterns of sunlight on the branches to make their games. They played games of pirate ships and tree houses and all sorts of adventures. The older children just climbed up and up, to show how high and how brave they were.

The little holly tree looked at the smooth strong branches of the beech tree and then she looked at her own branches, that grew so close together they did not allow the sunlight through. She knew that the children could never play with her like that. She hung her branches even lower and tried not to mind about the children ignoring her. But she felt so lonely and so ugly.

As the shadows grew longer the children packed up their games and went home. They were all laughing and talking to each other as they walked through the forest. The holly tree watched them disappearing and felt sad all over again. It looked such fun having all those children climbing and playing their games with you. Maybe she should try and grow a bit more and see if they would come and play with her then. But no matter how hard she tried she could not grow any faster.

A few weeks later, the children came back into the forest. This time they carried bags and sticks and sacks. They stood around the great oak trees that stood next to each other over in the far corner of the forest. They threw the sticks up into the branches of the great oak trees and started to collect the acorns that fell down. They were talking about how they would feed them to the pigs that lived in the farmer's field in the village. The big old black and white sow would come and rub her back along the fence when the children fed her the acorns. When they had filled all their boxes and sacks, they packed everything up and went back to their homes.

The holly tree looked at her tiny hard green berries. You could hardly see them, hidden in between the hard prickly dark green leaves. She wondered how she could get the children to come and play with her, but, try as she might, she could only grow dark green prickly leaves and lots of thin branches that grew too close together.

Then the wind began to grow a little harder and a little colder. The sun didn't come and shine her warm smile into the forest so much. The leaves on all the other trees began to change into the most beautiful colours you could imagine. The forest looked as if someone had thrown pots of paint all over it. There were reds and yellows and browns and oranges and even some colours that looked like purple. Now the children came and danced through the piles of leaves that had been blown into corners by the wind. They collected all the sticks and twigs that had been thrown down by the trees and made a small fire surrounded by big stones. They were very careful to make sure that the fire could not hurt the forest. And they all danced and cooked chestnuts from the sweet chestnut tree that grew in another corner of the forest.

None of the children came near to the little holly tree. They did not collect her twigs and leaves because they were too sharp and prickly to touch. Now she really hated her leaves and branches. She longed to be like the other trees in the forest and make the children want to come and play with her. But nothing was going to change the shape of her leaves or the size of her branches. She could only ever be a holly tree because that was what she was.

The little holly tree started to feel so sad and lonely that she did not notice the wind getting colder and colder. She did not notice the small white flecks that started to come with the wind. She did not notice how bare all the other trees looked, with their leaves fallen and blown around in the mud. She only thought of how many times the children came into the forest and did not come to visit her.

One day, when she was feeling very sad and sorry indeed, she heard the children come back into the forest. This time she did not look to see where they were going to play. She closed her ears and eyes tight so that she did not know they were there. She did not see them walking towards her. She did not hear them saying, 'What beautiful red berries the holly tree has now, and look how dark and green she stands, against all the other trees with no leaves any more.'

Then the children began to dance round the little holly tree. They sang songs about how beautiful her berries were, and how all through the winter she would give food and shelter to all the birds hiding underneath her thick dark leaves and fine tangled branches. They danced and danced round her and sang and sang until she started to look up and smile. Then she rustled her leaves and shook her berries a little more. The children had come to see her. They were singing about her and dancing round her in circles. The children began to thank the holly tree for giving them some of her leaves and berries to put in their homes to brighten the winter. The holly felt so proud that now she was the only tree in all the forest that the children came to and she gladly gave them some of her leaves and berries to take home.

The next spring, when the children came to visit the chestnut trees, she enjoyed watching their games. She smiled to herself and thought, 'It will be my turn again soon enough,' and she never felt sad again.

Interpreting the story of The Little Holly Tree

Write a list of your own impressions and thoughts on this story. Does your list include the following areas:

+ loneliness
+ wanting to be special
+ feeling different
+ starting a new stage in life
+ being impatient
+ being confused
+ experiencing prejudice
+ starting a new school
+ reaching puberty?

Compare your list to this one and see how similar your ideas are.

Write a brief summary of one of your own experiences which fits in with one theme from this story.

Does this exercise make any difference to your understanding of that experience? Hopefully, using the story, you have learned a little more from that experience, even if it happened many years ago. The learning never stops because it is always possible to see things from a new perspective.

The following possible interpretations of the little holly tree story can be worked through in any order according to their relevance to your life and your child's life. Many of the themes overlap, just as real-life experiences overlap each other. Please read them and adapt them to your own and your child's experiences.

Loneliness

The holly tree looks around and sees all the other trees in the forest. She tries to communicate with them but they do not want to reply. We can all feel like this at times, when we are surrounded by people and lots of things are happening but somehow we are not being heard.

Children can feel like this very easily in a family that is busy and full of activity, focusing on certain priorities that are seen as the most important to the welfare of the family. But somewhere deep inside the family one person is not being heard. And they feel lonely. They may try everything to get attention and with repeated failure they gradually withdraw. The holly tree ruffles her leaves and shakes her branches, but she learns that she is not able to get the attention she wants and she gradually withdraws from being interested in what else is happening in the forest. Why should she be interested in anyone else if they are not interested in her?

Eventually the children do come and dance round her and she learns self-acceptance. In many ways this is too easy and the story suggests that one simple gesture will put everything right. But our holly tree is very wise because she is a tree. Children may need more explanation and understanding to enable them to heal quickly. Children do have a similar kind of wisdom to the holly tree, they do not get caught up in endless hypothetical justifications for things, they see things in very simple terms and the holly tree's simplicity is representing the child in this way.

This story can help a child to understand that they do not need to feel lonely, but it can also be used to help a child explain how they feel.

Wanting to be special

Another interpretation of this story could be that the children represent family, parents, and the holly tree is a child trying to get attention. She feels very lonely and her self-esteem is dropping all the time as she is more and more ignored. This could remind us, as parents, of the need to give regular and consistent attention to our children – but not to focus on them all the time, otherwise they become nothing more than performing seals in the family. However cute, do not fall into the trap of over-attention.

However, being aware of your child and all the progress they make in life, right from the beginning, is important, or like the holly tree, their sense of self will be diminished, resulting in a loss of self-worth and self-esteem. This is a problem because then they will do almost anything to attract attention. A naughty child is usually trying to attract attention, because any attention is better than nothing.

So, like a child starting anything new, the holly tree is very optimistic and enthusiastic and wants someone to notice her in the same way that she has started to notice those around her. She doesn't have a very strong sense of self yet, and is looking for a response from the other trees and the children, to see how she fits in. Her enthusiasm reminds me of young children who have not been thwarted in their development and some adults retain this fresh enthusiasm for new projects, ideas and adventures into old age. But equally a teenager can begin to experiment with identities and a developing sense of independence and adventure in their life. Both of these stages are essential for their development into adulthood.

Feeling different

Many children feel different at some stage of their life and there are a number of reasons why this can occur. The Little Holly Tree story illustrates the differences that exist but also shows that there is nothing wrong with them. The holly tree really dislikes herself because she feels different, and she does not see the value of her differences for a long time.

We are all dependent on other people to reflect our value back to us and such feedback is an essential part of our growing awareness of self, of who we are. The holly tree eventually learns that she, too, has value in her own way. It just takes her some time to be able to recognise her own special worth, and she is only able to do that through her value being recognised and rewarded by the children dancing round her and telling her how lovely she looks with her dark leaves when all the other trees are bare in the winter. The holly tree sees her dark evergreen leaves only as a disadvantage until the advantage is clearly shown to her. Most of the time we concentrate on looking at the disadvantages of our personalities and do not spend enough time thinking about the advantages.

Starting a new stage in life

The story can be used to illustrate the developmental stages of childhood, as follows:

- **Early childhood.** Initially in the story the little holly tree is suddenly awakened and looking around, getting to know her environment. In many ways she represents the *tabula rasa* model of the child, a blank surface on which life will write her story. She does not know what to expect and is full of hopeful and joyful expectation. Although most people do not really see the child as a blank surface, we do all acknowledge that the child is ready to learn everything they will need to survive. They are programmed to do so, and the majority of significant learning will have already taken place by the age of five years. This early stage is usually the template for future experience and interpretation. It establishes a sense of the 'normal'.

- **Mid childhood.** The holly tree was born some time ago but has gone through a higher transformation of consciousness. These types of transformation occur in children's lives in several ways. It is the fine-tuning of experience and success in the social world that takes place. There is a distinct change in the way a child views friends and friendship, moral dilemmas and many other aspects of their life at this age.

They begin to see other people as more than just available for their convenience, and deep and lasting friendships can begin at the age of about seven years old. Several developmental psychologists, such as Piaget and Bruner, have noted in children of this age a change in the level of awareness of those around them. Donaldson and Hughes saw it as the ability to think from the perspective of another, what Piaget called the ability to 'decentre'.

This transition does not happen in one go, it is a gradual process taking several years, but it is seen as a watershed in emotional development because it represents the ability to take responsibility. In other cultures this is the age when girls are expected to take care of the younger siblings while the mother deals with the new babies and other household duties. A boy is expected to take responsibility for a small group of cattle or donkeys or contribute in the work of the men.

In modern society these rites of passage are denied to our

children and there is very little marking this transition. Yet it should not be forgotten. This is the time when your child can really start to use stories to learn from because they can imagine themselves in the shoes of the character in the story. This represents a child's growing awareness of their experiential field and their place in it, and especially their ability to empathise.

♦ **Adolescence.** This is a stage where the child has to develop yet another sense of identity for themselves. They have to participate on a more equal level with adults and that can seem scary. Rather than being the little tree growing up, the holly tree is now big enough to compare herself with the other trees around her.

  The new sense of identity in adolescence is not just about physical changes, but also, and more importantly, about all the social and emotional changes which accompany it. Now the holly tree wants to participate in the activities in the forest but she doesn't really know how. To begin with all her attempts fail and she feels dejected and has a sense of failure. She withdraws rather than risk any more failure.

  In adolescence many of the tasks and changes feel like climbing Mount Everest and represent a major challenge for the young adult. They need support and encouragement to continue, just as the holly tree receives support and interest from the children and then is able to understand her place in the cycles of the forest. But the task remains her responsibility. The young adult will need to learn that they must find their own place, that it will not be offered to them as soon as they open their eyes to look for it.

Being impatient

Many children are very impatient and want to make things happen immediately. Yet, as Daniel Goleman suggests, waiting for the longer-term reward is often more satisfying and shows a level of maturity and restraint which is a sign of potential success in adult life. Accepting that everything has its time and its season is important. The holly tree has to wait for the full cycle of seasons from spring right through to the winter in order to find out what her reward is. She finds it hard to wait and gives up hope, giving in to feelings of low self-esteem and hopelessness. However, recognising that the goodies do arrive if you wait for them gives her a new and more mature perspective on life and she is then able to recognise the value and pleasure of waiting and anticipation.

Being confused

In this story the holly tree has certain expectations of how she will be received and when they are not fulfilled she is confused and hurt. She feels somehow that she is in the wrong place and nothing about her experiences seem to be good. In fact, nothing about herself seems to be good. Children sometimes experience this in a number of ways and at different times in their lives. It is usually concerned with other changes in life which are addressed elsewhere in this analysis.

Experiencing prejudice

This story could lead into a discussion of racism or disability. It shows that even if one person seems to be different in a very obvious way, we are in fact all different. All the trees are different in many ways, but they are all trees. Differences should be valued and, of course, are valued by enlightened people who teach acceptance of all others whatever they have done or appear to be. It is our very humanity which makes us more similar than any minor detail of difference. The holly tree is still a tree even if she doesn't lose her leaves in winter like all the other trees. But, like children who experience unkindness and ignorance from others, she begins to hate her leaves and her flowers and her branches and everything that makes her herself. She sees only the disadvantages in them all, compared to the other trees. This loss of self-esteem is experienced by children on so many levels and in so many ways that the parent could apply it to any experiences that the child may have had.

It's not until much later in the year that the holly tree begins to understand the value of her differences and learns to appreciate their contribution to the children who come to the forest, thus keeping the continuity of their relationship with the forest going even through the winter. She is the one they choose to turn to when the weather becomes too cold to visit the forest any more. She is their reminder of their love of the forest and all the good things in life that await in the new spring. Thus the cycles of life and living are experienced through the seasons of the forest.

Starting a new school

This can feel very intimidating, especially if it is a new area and there will not be anyone to go with on the first day. Of course, most sensitive teachers will elect a child to take care of the new one until they find their own way, but sometimes this is not enough. The story of The Little Holly Tree could be used to help a child understand and interpret their fears about such changes.

The important thing is not to make the child feel silly for being unsure of the unknown but to help them to see that the unknown is a new opportunity for learning and exploring. What we learn from the holly tree is that, to begin with, no one really is interested in her. The other trees (or other children in a new school) have been around for longer. They know who's who and what's what and they don't need to take her into account. So she feels increasingly lonely. This may only be for the first week for the child in a new school, but a week can seem like an awfully long time when you are going through change.

As the holly tree's year progresses, she starts to retreat more and more and loses her self-esteem and her enthusiasm. Her confidence and interest has not been responded to by those around. Then she is surprised when suddenly the children come and visit her and choose her to dance around. This teaches the child that they cannot be the centre of attention and they have to wait to find their niche in the new situation. The holly tree learns to be patient and wait her turn. She learns that she does not have to be the centre of the attention all the time but that everyone should have their turn. She learns that by waiting she will have her time of recognition and that each of the trees has their special quality which may not always be obvious but at the right time it is clear how each tree provides the forest with all that it needs, and also for the children who visit it.

Reaching puberty

The story of The Little Holly Tree can also represent transformation from one stage of life to another. One of the most significant transformations is that of puberty. Because we live in a society where sex is still largely an under-discussed issue other than in terms of its censorship or exploitation, it is a potential emotional minefield for our children in terms of their changing sense of self.

The story also shows the importance of not conforming to everyone else. The essential differences in all of us are part of the richness of our humanity. We need all of those differences. The holly tree's thick sharp leaves could be seen as a disability that a child has. However, what we don't have in one area, we make up for in another. Some of the most disabled children are also the greatest sources of spontaneous affection and joy at living. Their differences are a lesson to us all.

Summary

Almost as soon as a child opens their eyes, they begin to learn about their family and environment so that they can survive and become part of it. It is essential not to over-protect your child against experiences that will help them to learn and grow, but there are key stages in a child's life which present challenges. These challenges provide the optimum opportunities for parents to help their children to understand themselves and the world and become more emotionally intelligent.

Questions to discuss with your child

1   What would have happened if the holly tree had got *all* the attention every time the children came into the forest?
2   What did she have to learn?
3   Was it easy for her to learn this lesson?
4   Could she have learned this lesson any other way?
5   What could the other trees in the forest have done to help her?

CHAPTER 11

The Fox and the Blue Grapes

Long ago, deep in the forest, there grew a vine. She was a most unusual vine and grew the most unusual blue grapes. She loved the days in the sunshine in her little corner of the forest and spoke to the trees around her. They were her friends. They loved to laugh together and rustle their leaves.

Many animals would come to taste the sweet blue grapes of the vine. Squirrels came to play in her branches and made her tickle with their tiny little claws. Birds would come and sing to her. The wind would come and flutter her leaves and share his thoughts with her. She loved them all.

One day a fox was walking through the forest. The vine saw the fox. His sleek red coat and long bushy tail glinted in the sunlight. She saw how handsome he was. He played games and did tricks for her. He started to visit the vine often. The vine would look forward to his arrival.

She loved to watch him play, rolling around on the ground. He would roll over and over, as if he would never stop. It made her laugh. She watched eagerly each day to see what games he would invent next. He made her laugh even more than the squirrels did with their tiny claws. Even more than the wind did with the stories of his travels. Even more than the birds did with their funny little songs.

The vine grew to love the fox and gave him big bunches of her beautiful blue grapes. These were the sweetest grapes that the fox had ever tasted in his life and he began to long for the grapes. He wanted them, more and more. If he went off into the forest, he would always hurry back and play under the vine and she would give him her fruit to show how much she loved him. And when he lay down to rest after playing his games for her, she would stroke his fur with her tendrils and soothe him to sleep under her branches.

Soon the fox started to feel worried that someone else might want to take the grapes from the vine. He didn't want her to share her grapes with the squirrels and the birds any more. He wanted the vine all for himself.

The thought inside his head grew and grew until he could not bear the idea of anyone else wanting *his* blue grapes, because that is how he now thought of them. He forgot that the grapes were a gift from the vine. He forgot that the vine gave them to him in return for the games that made her laugh. These thoughts made him very scared. And very angry. The more he thought these thoughts, the more scared and angry he became. He still came to the vine every day but he did not play so much. Still the vine gave him her beautiful big blue grapes, as much as he could eat.

One day the fox came to the vine and said nothing at all. He did not play or try to make the vine laugh. He tried to chase away the birds that sang high in her branches. He could not reach them and they laughed at him. This made the fox very angry indeed. He threw stones at them to make them fly away. Then he snatched at some grapes hanging down above his head. He took all that he wanted. He forgot to thank the vine.

The vine watched sadly. She missed the singing of the birds in her branches. When the fox had eaten all the grapes that he could manage, and was very full, too full to move, he lay down. The vine wanted to stroke his fur to make him feel happy again. He was too angry and moved away. The vine couldn't reach him.

As he slept, the fox felt cold and unhappy. He had many bad dreams. He missed the soft tendrils stroking his fur as he slept. He became more and more angry with the vine because she did not stroke his fur any more. He forgot that she could not move her feet like he could. He forgot that it was he who had gone to sleep too far away for her to reach him.

Then the fox had an idea. He would show everyone that the vine was his and belonged to him. As he stuck the knife into the bark of the vine she cried out and begged him to stop. She tried to stroke him and to offer him grapes but he ignored her. He was determined to make sure that no one else would get his vine and that no one else would want her. The vine could feel her sap dripping from the cuts that he made with the knife. She thought that she would die.

When the fox had finished he smiled to himself. His name now showed proudly on the bark of the vine. He could hear the sadness of the vine but he ignored her. She was his vine now. He lay down and went to sleep, close to the vine. He waited for the vine to stroke him but she did not. She was busy making new bark to cover up the cuts that he had made and to stop her sap from dripping away. She kept her tendrils to herself.

When the fox woke up he reached out for a bunch of grapes. But the vine had not got many bunches left because the fox had been so greedy. There was one beautiful big bunch hanging high up in the branches of the vine. He told the vine to give him those grapes. He forgot that she could not move like he could. Then he got angry again and threw sticks and stones at the bunch of grapes. The grapes began to smash as the stones hit them, until the bunch was just a mushy mess. But still they did not fall to the ground.

Then the fox got very angry indeed and went off into the forest on his own, to find a new vine to play tricks for. 'I'll show that vine that I don't need her any more,' he thought to himself.

When the fox left, all the birds and the squirrels came back to the vine and she started to laugh again. The wind dropped by and told her more stories. The squirrels brought their babies and showed them how to make the vine giggle as they tickled her with their sharp little claws. And the scars of his name healed over until there was hardly a trace.

The fox wandered far and near but all he could find were vines with ordinary purple and green grapes. Nowhere could he find a vine with beautiful blue grapes that were so big and so sweet as his vine.

He wandered for many days until he suddenly realised how much he missed his vine. He went back through the forest and found her still growing beautiful and strong. He looked for the mark of his name but it was not there. She had grown new bark to cover over the marks he had made. When the fox saw that he became even angrier and started to cut the vine down. He hacked away at her branches and trunk and made more cuts than you could imagine. The vine cried out and begged him to stop: 'I will grow lots of grapes for you if you play for me and make me laugh again.'

She pleaded with the fox but he was too angry. He could not

hear her words. The vine stopped saying anything and silently waited for him to stop cutting her.

The wind was wandering through the forest. He heard the cries of the vine and thought how sad she sounded. Then he heard her silence. He loved the vine. He blew hurriedly through the forest bending all the trees as he went. 'Hurry, hurry,' all the trees called out to the wind as he passed them by.

When he saw what the fox was doing he called to the fox to stop cutting the vine down. The fox didn't listen to him either. Then the wind sucked in his cheeks as far as they could go and started to blow. He blew as hard as he could. The fox tried to carry on cutting the vine down but the wind was too strong for him. It blew him over and sent him tumbling over and over across the ground. Then the wind lifted the fox right up into the air and carried him far away, to another forest where there were no more vines. He told the fox never to come back to that forest again.

The fox was very sad to begin with. Then he told himself and his new friends in the new forest that the blue grapes had never been that special and that he would find something just as sweet to eat in this forest. And he played and made everyone laugh and they thought that it must be true, that the blue grapes were never that good anyway. He was such a jolly good fox.

The vine grew strong again. All the trees around her helped. Very soon she was as big and beautiful as ever. Sometimes she felt very sad and missed the fox playing under her branches but then she would remember how he had chased away her friends, and had carved her bark till the sap dripped, and smashed her grapes with stones. And worst of all she remembered how he had tried to cut her down. Then she was glad that he had gone. Now she could play with the squirrels and the birds whenever she wanted. She could grow her big beautiful blue grapes and give them to all her friends. She would live happily ever after.

Interpreting the story of The Fox and the Blue Grapes

This story has many interpretations, so, as before, see how many you can think of. My list includes:

- domestic violence
- bullying

- jealousy
- fear and anger
- falling out with best friends
- cognitive dissonance and self-deception
- understanding love
- listening and not listening
- trusting and not trusting.

Domestic violence

This is a theme which is very difficult to discuss and yet is a common experience for many children. Our story does not pass judgement on the characters but it does illustrate some of the complexities of the issue; for instance, the connection between love and fear, and how they can overlap in ways that become destructive if our inner voices are based on fear interpretations of life.

The fox does not have a very strong intrinsic sense of self and is dependent on others to feel good and valued. He has learned how to make people laugh and delighted with him but he is too needy to be able to cope with any competition and his insecurity kicks in with a fear of loss. He cannot accept that the vine is able to love many (people) without detracting from her love for him. He is so busy extracting the love he needs that he forgets to return her love in positive ways that recognise her inner self. The hurt this inflicts on her makes her withdraw slightly, as a self-protection mechanism. This makes him feel even more insecure and the vicious cycle continues with the fox feeling more and more threatened, expressed through anger which eventually gets out of control. In the end he destroys the very love which he so desperately wanted to keep, and like Aesop's fox, decides that the blue grapes weren't that good after all. He is sent away by the wind, representing whatever force does end such relationships, i.e. the law, extended family and friends, therapists, etc.

A child who is faced by violence can be helped to understand what is happening and not feel that they are somehow to blame by recognising that the motivation for violence and aggression is always fear, therefore the perpetrator is the biggest victim and can be forgiven. They will lose more in the long run. By releasing the guilt and fear attached to violence, it is possible to grow from the experience, through forgiveness.

Bullying

This is very similar to domestic violence, but usually refers to a situation outside the family. Very often the victim of bullying doesn't understand why they are being picked on, but at an unconscious level they are fearful characters who do not have strong internal boundaries, and who in their own way will give out messages that they are easy targets. The vine is unable to move and this represents her vulnerability. She is passive and allows others to come and take from her in return for very little except the feeling of being needed. The fox takes this to an extreme which nearly destroys her and she learns to be more careful with her generosity, restricting it to those she can trust.

Jealousy

The fox is fearful of losing his control and influence over the vine and is obsessed with keeping all her qualities, as expressed by the blue grapes, for himself. This is common in relationships where one partner has low self-esteem and is using the other as a scaffold or prop. He is so jealous of her affection for others that he would do anything to keep them away and have all the blue grapes for himself, even if that means making the vine unhappy and actually less able to produce so many grapes. By restricting her, the fox is destroying the very qualities which he is so desperate to have. This often happens in relationships where one or both partners are too insecure and low in self-esteem that they are dependent on others, yet destroy the other in their desperate sense of need, thereby making themselves feel better or superior, but also triggering fear as their support system withdraws and disintegrates.

Fear and anger

Fear is the basis of the destruction of what could have been a very mutually fulfilling and rewarding relationships between the fox and the vine. Fear is the opposite of love and the source of all negative experiences. Anger is one of the most common manifestations of fear, a response which easily builds on itself until it becomes out of control. Anger is an attempt to control the source of fear but it usually has the opposite effect by destroying love and trust. Thus the fox becomes more fearful as he becomes more angry and is unable to control the vine because she has feelings which he is failing to recognise in his desperation. He is trying to manipulate her for his own needs but she is an individual and therefore has her own needs, responses and understanding, which he cannot control. It is important to recognise this in everyone we come into contact with, both in relationships at home and at work.

Falling out with best friends

For a child this can feel like the worst thing to happen, especially if their home life is secure and stable. Separation and loss is something that we must all experience in order to understand that love is the absence of fear. Perhaps the way in which the 'best friendship' between the fox and vine is spoilt is similar to a very jealous and possessive situation which the child has had difficulty coping with. Or perhaps the child is the jealous friend who needs to see what they are doing in a detached format so that they can think about the possible outcome of their behaviour.

Cognitive dissonance and self-deception

These are more or less the same thing and occur when we tell ourselves and others something which we know is not true, but we will find an excuse to justify it and eventually believe the new story. The dissonance is the sense of conflict that we feel about the known lie and we change our belief system in order to make the lie more comfortable, i.e. no longer a lie but the truth. The fox expresses his cognitive dissonance when he rejects the grapes and says they were not as sweet as he thought they were to begin with, because he cannot bear the truth, which is that he was rejected by the vine and that he tried to destroy her. It is his own inability to recognise and face his own fear which becomes a destructive force in his life and gives him ever more reasons [1] withdraw from life. The vine understands own life worse than hers, because she has she had before he came along, and althou a little from time to time, she is glad to h control games.

Understanding love

The vine understands that love is giving and not expecting something in return. It is also living without fear, and she is generous in this part of her life to all who come near to her. The fox does not and is not able to love the vine or anyone else because he is too emotionally dependent on approval and has a low self-esteem that means he does not love himself. In many ways he is like Keith in the case studies in earlier chapters. Our story clearly shows that the vine loved the fox and would have continued to do so if he had valued her and respected her life which existed before he came along, which was what he had been attracted to and what he became insanely jealous of, to the point of destruction. The story also shows the vine as non-vindictive and forgiving, a sign of how much love she has and how little fear there is in her life. Fear can attack love but a love without fear cannot be destroyed because it is the stronger emotion in the end. She trusts the wind and the other small creatures who come to play with her and this heals all the wounds that the fox has inflicted.

Listening and not listening

The fox listens to what the vine says and to the others who come to visit her but he hears them in a distorted way because of his own insecurity and fear. He hears them as threats, as beings who will come between him and his need fulfilment from the vine. To the fox his interpretation is the only real one because it is based on his perceptual bias of fear. We don't know the childhood experiences of the fox, we just see the result of the damage in his life and how his fear-based perceptual bias prevents him ever finding contentment or success in his life. He just runs from one disaster to another and never takes responsibility for his actions. This is why it is so important to love yourself in a simple acceptance and forgiving way that allows you to take responsibility and live without fear in your life.

Trusting and not trusting

The fox is unable to trust anything or anyone in his life because he cannot trust himself. He has very weak boundaries and they are easily wiped out by the power of his fear. He behaves in ways which he finds disgusting but experiences such distress with himself that he convinces himself that the vine deserved it and was a fake, less good than she was supposed to be.

By contrast, the vine trusts the fox and gives him her fruit which represents her love for him. She is shocked by the changes in him and sad for his fear, but she cannot reach him because he also listens with the perceptions of fear. Nothing can get past that because he protects himself with massive barriers based on that fear, allowing little through except his expectations, which he fulfils for himself regardless of the efforts of the vine. Whose loss is the greater?

The fox's lack of trust that the vine would always give him as many grapes as he could eat, if he would only let her live and continue all the parts of her life, shows how important it is for parents to teach their children to trust and for parents to be trustworthy for their children with honesty and openness. Megan (see page 46) in the end will learn that she cannot trust Keith and will start to keep parts of her life from him. He will fulfil his own fear there too because he cannot believe that anyone can be trusted, because he cannot trust himself. The fox cannot trust anyone else until he has learned to trust himself and this is the key to trust.

This aspect relates also to Violet (see next story). She held on to the trust in her instincts, thanks to Old Mags and in spite of her parents. She did not lose sight of the power of love and belief in the inner self because she had learned to trust, as had the vine.

The wind represents a position of authority, the law, a friend, etc., and his influence on the situation restores her trust in herself very quickly. One mistake does not destroy your self-confidence, but it will teach you valuable lessons.

CHAPTER 12

Violet

'Violet, Violet can you hear me?'

The voice was so sweet and so gentle, it sang like the wind playing through hollow wood. The little girl stirred in her sleep but did not wake up.

'Trouble is coming to the forest, Violet, and you must save us all.'

Still Violet did not wake up.

'We will tell you when it is time. Don't forget, Violet, don't forget.'

Then the singing stopped.

Violet woke up. She rubbed her eyes and looked around. She was sure that someone had been talking to her but she was alone, as usual, in the forest. The sun was getting low. There were all sorts of stories about the spirits of the trees that lived there. Most people said it was all nonsense but they did not go into the forest at night either. Violet hurried home.

'Why are you so late?' her mother demanded as she hurried in through the door.

'I fell asleep by the silver tree with the twisted trunk. I came home as soon as I woke up. I was dreaming.' Violet spoke very softly, almost whispering the last words. 'I dreamed that someone was talking to me, asking me to save the forest.'

'I told you never to go back into the forest, especially not back to the tree with the twisted trunks.'

But when Violet asked her mother why, she became more and more angry.

That night her father came home looking especially pleased. He hugged Violet as he came through the door.

'We're going to be rich, Violet, we're going to be rich. We're going to have all the lovely things that other people have instead of always having to scrape a living out of the fields and the forest.'

And he danced around the tiny living room, bumping into the table and chairs and knocking over the candlesticks.

Violet looked at her father with disbelief. He was never this happy and he usually came home ready to be angry with her because of something she had done or not done. Her mother called out from the kitchen at the back of the house.

'Tell me what has been decided then.'

'We're going to sell the forest and the lumber company will pay us and do all the work and then tell us how to start all over again. It was agreed at the village council meeting.'

Violet's mother came out of the kitchen, rubbing the flour off her hands with a cloth. 'Does that mean I won't have to work in the fields and kitchen all day?'

'Yes my love, we'll be able to buy whatever we want. The lumber company are going to set up a shop in the village and we can buy things from them.'

'What's a shop and what's a buy?' asked Violet.

As her father began to explain, Violet became even more puzzled.

'Then why do we need this? The village council makes sure that everything is shared out fairly and that everyone is fed and sheltered for the year. Then we have all the festivals for each part of the year and the gifts from the forest.' Her father held up his hand but Violet carried on, 'And why do they want to buy the forest? They can't take it away.'

'Oh why are you asking so many questions,' he said crossly, 'they will cut the trees down and take them away. What do you think?'

Violet burst into tears and screamed, 'No. No. They can't, they mustn't.'

Her father was angry now. 'Go to your room,' he ordered, 'and don't come down until you stop these silly ideas about the forest being your friend. It's just a bunch of silly old trees.'

Violet could not understand why her father and mother did not love the forest as she did. She lay on her bed, buried her face in the covers and cried herself to sleep. As she slept she dreamed that the forest was calling to her.

'Go and see Old Mags. She will tell you what to do.' The voice flew on the wind, through the window, into Violet's dreams.

The following morning Violet woke up and knew what she

must do. She climbed out of bed and left the cottage before her mother and father were up. It was still dark as she crept through the village and out to the little hut at the edge of the forest where Old Mags lived. No one really spoke to Old Mags but they all sent for her when they were ill. She knew the wisdom of the plants in the forest and she could deliver a child without any pain for the mother. Everyone in the village was really a bit scared of her but they could not admit it. Violet trembled and shivered as she went. 'It's the cold,' she told herself, reluctant to admit that it was really the thought of going to see Old Mags on her own.

Old Mags was waiting for Violet and opened the door for her. She listened while Violet told her what had happened.

'Shall we take some lemonade out into the garden and watch the sun rise? Then I'll tell you a story about the forest when it was very young.'

They sat down on a rickety old bench in the corner of Mags' garden, watching the sky turn pink and the day getting brighter and brighter. 'I watch the sun rise every day. Then I know that it is a new day, a new birth and new things will happen.' They sat in silence until the sun had risen higher than the trees. Then, enjoying the warmth of the sun, Violet listened while Mags told her the legend of Wildwood.

'Once upon a time, long ago when stories were just beginning, there lived a young man called Woodwind. His mother had named him after the gentle calling sounds he made in his cradle whenever he heard the wind blowing through the trees. He loved to go walking far off, to see what he could see and hear what he could hear. He feared nothing and was always happy. He knew that shadows only make the light seem brighter.

One day he walked for a long time, to a very distant part of the land. As he walked he heard a beautiful sound coming from deep in the trees, calling to him. It made him think of love and sadness, beauty and death. It spoke of time, the seasons, and a wisdom that goes beyond all of this. He kept following the sounds until he came to a small group of trees deep in the heart of the forest. In the centre was a beautiful young woman, singing and dancing among the trees, her long green and gold hair swirling and twirling around her as she moved.

Woodwind stayed behind the trees, listening and watching her for a very long time, until the shadows also joined hands and danced with the girl, until the light was almost gone. Then she stood still, lifted her arms up towards the night sky and slipped away into the trees at the other side of the clearing. Woodwind tried to follow her but as soon as he reached the centre of the clearing she had disappeared. He looked everywhere but could not find her. He felt lost and saddened by her disappearance. Finally, realising how dark the night had become and that he no longer knew which direction he had come from, Woodwind lay down in the centre of the clearing and went to sleep. As he slept he dreamed that all the trees around the edge of the clearing had come to life and were standing over him. At first they were very angry with him and shook their fists to drive him away. Then the young woman returned and waved her arms around in a circle above her head. And the others started to dance round him, slowly and softly so as not to wake him. All night they circled him until the first light of dawn came creeping over the tops of the trees. Then they all quietly slipped away into the trees.

When Woodwind woke, he rubbed his eyes and looked around. Just the circle of trees. The sun rose in the sky and started to warm him and he sat and wondered if the dreams had been real. Just then, the young woman slipped out from behind a tree.

"Why are you here? It is not allowed for humans to come to the place of the dancing trees."

"I have never heard of such a place. I was walking and I heard your singing. I had to follow it. It called to me. But when you stopped singing, I could not find you. I could not see where you had gone to."

"Humans cannot hear the songs of the Dryads, they only hear the rustling of our leaves or the creaking of our branches." Her head tilted to one side in thoughtfulness and her hair floated in the breeze.

"Your song is the most beautiful song that I have ever heard. I want to listen to it for the rest of my life. Will you sing for me again?"

The woman made a deep rich sound like the sound of hollow wood being drummed. Woodwind realised that she was laughing and he laughed with her.

"What is your name, young man?"

"I am called Woodwind after the noises I made when I was young."

"With a name like that you must be able to hear the songs of the Dryads. You are welcome. It is many years since humans and Dryads were able to work together and hear each others' words. My name is Silvrine and this is my tree. I carry all the seasons of the tree in me."

She pointed to a tall graceful silver birch tree, with beautiful silver bark and light fluttering leaves that hung down from its branches. Then Woodwind could see that her hair drifted as the leaves moved and fluttered in the gentle breeze, green for the spring and golden for the autumn. Silvrine and Woodwind sat and talked for many days. Each night she would leave him and return to her tree, for a Dryad will die if they leave their tree for too long. Woodwind slept each night in the circle of trees, guarded and protected by all the other Dryads. As the days went by Silvrine told of the history of humans and Dryads. Of how her great great grandfather had followed the humans into battle, had fought on the side of the Druids, the Men of Oak to protect the forests. But the humans made too many battles and the Dryads lost too many of their kind. Once the Dryad has died, the tree will become an ordinary tree with no spirit and it will die soon after, a long slow death.

As Woodwind and Silvrine talked, they grew to love each other more and more.

"But if I leave my tree to live with you, our children will be of the forest and I will die the death of a human. My tree will die when I do."

"Then you must never leave your tree for me."

Woodwind and Silvrine talked for many more months and the days became cold. The Dryads covered Woodwind with their dead leaves to protect him, and threw down branches for shelter. They gave him nuts to eat and cared for him as one of their own. But Silvrine and Woodwind became more and more sad each evening as she had to leave him.

Eventually they went to the elders, the Dryads of the Great Oaks that stood sentinel over the whole forest. Oakhorn, the oldest, wisest Dryad in the forest, listened to their story and his wise old heart went out to them. He alone remembered the love between humans and Dryads from long ago.

Oakhorn knew that there were special times when a Dryad could leave their tree. But only for love. He saw the love that Woodwind and Silvrine shared but his heart was heavy, for the children of men and Dryads must also live in and love the forest if they are to thrive. And humans have short memories. Silvrine would die as a human sooner than Woodwind, but could return to her tree after twenty years and never leave it again. There she could live as the tree for the full life of a Dryad, which is many hundreds of years.

Oakhorn thought very hard about the future and what it might mean to the forest. The Dryads had chosen to keep away from humans because they did not understand their love of fighting and death. Dryads only love the seasons and the creatures that live in their boughs. Eventually he decided to tell them what he knew. He called to them.

"Silvrine, it is true that Dryads may not leave their tree for long. What is also true from long ago is that they may if it is for love. But you must return to your tree for one month every year and you may only leave for twenty years. After that you must never leave again. Your tree will not die if you return. You can choose what you wish to do."

Silvrine and Woodwind looked at each other and the love in their hearts spoke for them both. "I will do this. It is not such a short time." Silvrine held out her hand to Woodwind and they danced a little together around Oakhorn's mighty presence.

Silvrine nodded. "There will be many children who can keep Woodwind as he grows old."

Oakhorn shook his head slowly. "You may have but one child only. This child will have many more children. They will care for both of you."

And so Silvrine and Woodwind stayed together and had a son whom they called Wildwood. Each winter, Silvrine returned to her tree for one month. Wildwood grew up in the forest and everything they needed was provided by the trees. The Dryads would come out and dance with him in the evenings, and teach him of their gifts. The chestnuts and cobnuts would give him food, the mighty oak would give him wood to make shelters from, the willows that grew along the bank of the river which ran through the forest would give him boughs to make baskets.

When he became a young man, Silvrine took him to one side and told him what must happen. "Soon I must leave you. My time as a human has passed and I must return to my tree for ever. I have lived to see you grow into a man and I will always be with you as you live in the forest. I will watch you as you grow older and wiser. But now you must go and find yourself a love of your own. Bring her here to live. Your father will teach you how to grow food that you will need for your children. The forest will always provide for you and your children and their children but you must teach them all about the Dryads and never let them cut the trees. You must celebrate with the forest for each harvest it gives. When you need wood, the trees will give you their branches with the wind. Never never cut the living trees for you will be cutting your cousins, your family, your brothers and sisters of the forest. You will have many children and live a happy life if you choose carefully. Go my son, the birds of the forest will bring me word of you on your adventure." And she kissed Wildwood for the last time as his mother.

Wildwood shed many tears as he walked through the forest. Where they fell a small plant grew, with pale mauve flowers. The trees showed him the way back to the land of humans as he walked through them, touching each one as he passed in greeting. As he passed by Oakhorn, he heard the huge old oak sigh and he reached out and held his hand against its bark for a long time. He felt the love and wisdom of his friend and guardian of the forest. Then he knew that he must go and do as his mother told him.

A few weeks later, the birds brought the message that he had reached a village and met a young woman. Her family had taken him in and taught him the ways of humans. Silvrine sighed a long sigh. Her twenty years was ended and she knew that she must leave Woodwind in human form for ever. They stood with their arms entwined around each other for a very long time, next to Silvrine's tree. Woodwind couldn't bear to be parted from Silvrine. As they stood there their feet became roots and their arms became branches that danced and swayed with the wind. And gradually they both became one with Silvrine's tree. It was something that had never happened before, a human taking the form of a Dryad, and even Acorn watched with wonder at the power of love to transform those who love each other.

Wildwood returned to the forest with Bryony, his bride. They walked through the forest and all the Dryads welcomed Bryony. Eventually they came to the clearing and saw the trees, twisted and twined around each other. He sat at the foot of the tree and told his parents of his love. He heard the rustle of their leaves, the haunting sounds of their great hearts that echoed throughout the whole forest, and knew they were together.

Then he made a garland of the pale mauve flowers that grew all around the clearing and hung it all around the great trees that were his parents. Each year, at the same time, he made the garland of flowers and gave thanks to his parents for their protection. Bryony called them violets after her own mother.

And for each gift that the forest gave to Wildwood and Bryony, they thanked the forest with a celebration of dance and songs that his mother had taught him. Wildwood and Bryony had many children and lived well within the forest. They were careful to teach their children all that Silvrine had told Wildwood, so that the trees were never cut. The village became known as Wildwood, after their father who had taught them to love the forest and live in peace with all the animals. Everyone knew that as long as the trees were never cut, they would have all that they needed and could live happily ever after.

For many hundreds of years the stories were passed down from parent to child, that the forest would continue to provide all that they needed as long as they only took what they did need and no more, so that there was enough to go round for everyone, including all the animals, birds and insects that lived in the woods and round the fields.'

Violet sighed. She felt warmer now, in the sunshine. It was quite late. 'That's a lovely story, Mags. Is it true?'

'Does it feel true?' asked Mags. Violet nodded. 'Then believe what you feel inside. Now what does this story tell you about your father's news and your dreams at the roots of the old tree?'

Suddenly all made sense.

'That tree is Silvrine and Woodwind's tree, it was Silvrine calling to me but she can never leave her tree so she can only call to me. She knows what is to happen to the forest and she wants me to help. But how can I stop them? What can I do to stop my father and all the men in the village from cutting down the trees?' Violet started to cry at the thought of so much responsibility.

'Trust your instincts and you will know what to do,' said Old Mags. 'Go into the forest now and it will show you. Just open your eyes and see whatever you can see.'

When Violet heard of the new plans for the great old forest, she ran to the council and cried out that they must not forget the stories of the forest. They were true, surely everyone saw that the forest gave them all that they needed, the stories must be true. And what would happen to the festivals?

'Be quiet, Violet, everyone knows you are mad,' they said to her, 'go away and keep your old-fashioned ideas to yourself.'

Violet ran from one family to the next, crying out that they were wrong, that the trees would die and they would be left with nothing. They all turned away from her, pushing her with their hands and their hard hearts and stares.

Eventually, exhausted, Violet returned home, lay on her bed and cried. No one listened to Violet. Instead the people in the village started to argue about who owned the trees and the land, who would be in charge of the cutting and selling and who would be responsible for replanting and taking care of the new trees. The council argued for many days and nights. Eventually one family started to make itself in charge of the organising and they became the most experienced and knowledgeable about the trade practices. They negotiated the deals with the lumber company and eventually the trees were sold.

The noise of the machines cutting the trees was matched by the noise of the great trees hitting the ground and crushing the smaller ones in their path. Each day more and more trees were cut, and their songs at night became more and more sad. There was noise and dust everywhere.

Violet walked through the forest each night, just ahead of the cutting machines, touching each tree in turn and saying goodbye. The trees shook their branches sadly and gave her a little seed from each of their kind. Their sad songs whispered to her, 'Save us, grow our seeds so that we can live again.' And so Violet found a little corner of her garden and planted the seeds that the great

forest gave her. She wept for the sadness of their songs each night
and stopped playing with any of the other children in the village.
They just called her Crazy Violet and laughed at her even more
than before.

When the great cutting machines reached the two trees that
were twisted into one, a mighty crash was heard and the whole
tree split into two halves, then crumbled into dust, right in front
of the men driving the machine. They could not believe their eyes
and told the villagers that evening.

'See, I told you that the trees had hearts,' said Violet. 'That is the
tree of Silvrine and Woodwind. And now they are gone.'

But the woodsmen just laughed at Violet and said that it was
just a very old tree that was probably half dead already, eaten away
from the inside by insects. It was probably dangerous and would
have been blown over in the next big wind.

Each day the sky was full of more birds who had lost their
homes. The rabbits and squirrels soon came into the fields and
started to dig up the crops because they had lost their homes in
the forest. They began to eat the food that the villagers grew for
themselves because there was no food from the forest. The people
in the village had arguments about how they should stop the
rabbits eating their vegetables. Some people argued that they
should stop cutting down the forest and let it all grow back.
Others argued that they should just stop the rabbits eating the
food. 'How will we do that?' cried everyone at the meeting. 'The
rabbits are starving too.' They started killing the rabbits because
they were eating all the vegetables so fast that there would be none
left for the winter. Violet's father put his hand up when everyone
said that they couldn't possibly do this. 'We have no choice,' he
said. 'We will starve too if we do not kill them. Besides the
woodsmen said that rabbit stew is very tasty.'

The children of the village suddenly found that when they went
into the fields to play, all the rabbits ran away from them, so did
the squirrels and the voles, the frogs and the toads and the mice.
The children cried that they had nothing to play with any more.
The woodsmen arranged for the children to be given cloth
animals to play with. These animals were soft and warm, but they
did not move. The children missed their old friends.

There were no festivals any more. The families in the village stopped going out. If they did, they did not talk to each other as they had before. Instead they looked to see who had got a new chair in the house. The houses started to have fences put up around them and new gates on their fences. Other new possessions were brought into the forest. Some families seemed to get more than others. Some families were making their houses bigger, they were taking parts of the fields and common land to make bigger and bigger houses. They began to put up bigger and bigger fences, and bigger and bigger gates on their fences. And as the fences got higher and higher and the houses got bigger and bigger, the people laughed less and less and worried more and more. Nearly all the trees in the forest were cut down. The villagers started worrying how to heat their homes this winter, how to feed their animals from the nuts and how to bring the forest into their homes that winter.

Eventually the villagers went to see the village council and demanded to know what the woodsmen would do for them when the trees ran out. How would they feed their families and heat their homes and live their lives? And what about all the festivals? There was nothing to celebrate now. They needed their forest back. When were the woodsmen going to plant the new trees and give them enough food? Violet's father wrung his hands and agreed to go and ask the woodsmen.

They just laughed. 'We gave you the rewards for your forest, as you all agreed. it is up to you to sort out your own problems. We are busy and have new trees to cut.'

So the villagers sadly watched the woodsmen cut down the last few trees, until there were no more standing at all and the whole forest was silent.

Then the villagers went to see the village council but found them in tears. The woodsmen had gone. They had taken all their beautiful forest and left them with nothing. No one knew what to do. The whole village council meeting was silent with the sadness of the whole village for their beautiful forest. Then Violet, very quietly, said, 'Come and look next to my house.'

'It's just mad Violet again, what can she possibly know?'

'If you come and look, you will know. At least it is better than just sitting here in sorrow.'

The villagers heard her words and saw some wisdom in them

that they had not expected.

'What can you have, Violet?'

'I have the forest. I saved the forest while you were busy helping to cut it down.'

Then they all followed her. Violet led them to a small patch of ground near to the fence that had been put all around her house. She pointed with her finger, and there the villagers saw a little oak tree growing, and next to it a little chestnut tree, and a holly, and a yew, nut trees and beech trees. Willows. Ash trees. Silver birch trees, and more and more tiny baby trees. Then they realised that the little girl, at whom they had all laughed, had young trees growing from all the old trees in the forest.

Her tiny trees were carefully taken to the place where the old forest had once grown so proud and strong and the villagers made a festival to celebrate the planting of the new trees. The fences were taken down and used to keep the families warm in the winter and the land was shared with the animals again. The rabbits and squirrels used the soft warm fabric of the toy animals to make the nests for their babies until the trees were big enough to protect the animals as they once had done.

The people in the village started to smile and talk to each other again. They stopped looking to see what each family had got and started to share everything again.

The village council made Violet the new leader and asked her to forgive them for their laughter. She did immediately, she knew they would listen to her now. No one would ever again say that there was no such thing as a Dryad.

It took many years for the forest to grow back and many old people said that it was never the same again. The festival of the new planting became the most important festival of the village every year after that, and no one ever was allowed to forget the lesson they had learned.

Interpreting the story of Violet

What are your first thoughts and impressions of this story? It has many layers and includes a story within the story. It contains values, cautions, wisdom and myths. Does your list include any of the following:

- the importance of listening to older and younger people in society
- the importance of remembering old wisdom and teaching
- the importance of staying true to yourself and not following the majority
- the importance of parents listening to their children
- the abuse of power?

What areas of life could it be applied to:

- taking drugs or breaking other social rules
- fighting for what you believe in the face of criticism
- recognising the destructive nature of fear, pride and envy
- respecting all members of the family whatever their age
- learning to listen and communicate with open minds
- positive self-image for girls and womanhood
- respecting the environment
- learning to live without the newest designer labels
- the importance of contentment
- the destructiveness of greed and arrogance?

Listening to people of all ages

One of the clearest things in this story is that the only two people who do not follow the lead from the council are an old woman and a young girl. In our society these represent two of the most disempowered sections of the population and yet it is evident from this story that they have the clearest overview of the whole situation. Often it is the simplicity of childhood which can see straight to the centre of an issue and not become clouded with secondary considerations. Similarly older people have been through enough ups and downs to see what really matters.

In this story Old Mags is rather like the old wisewoman matriarchal figure in so many stories. She represents the wisdom of old age but also the third age of womanhood. The hag. Our culture sees this life as ugly and are afraid of it. The image of an old woman is not generally seen as positive unless it is in terms of how young and glamorous they are for their age. Both men and women need to embrace the beauty of wise woman images. She can be likened to Hecate in the story of Persephone and Demeter, the three women in that story representing the three stages of female development, the young girl who is learning to trust her instincts, the adult woman engaged in daily life and family considerations, and the old woman who has time to forget herself and exist in peace with her surroundings, knowing that she has lived each stage of her life fully meeting her potential. Old Mags is unaffected by the fear from the other villagers, she sees it for what it is and she is content to live her life and offer what she can to those who ask. She has found contentment and is in touch with her true self.

Violet is still trying to establish her individuality. She is very intuitive and a little bit unusual in this. Her parents see her as 'just a child' and assume that her dreams are nothing. She is being denied her true self. The story shows how hard it is for a child who is not fully listened to, who is ridiculed for being in tune with herself in a way that is misunderstood by those too busily engaged in a material life to notice beyond that. Her mother and father have lost touch with the part of themselves that experiences the beauty of natural living things and the joy of existence, they have become caught up in their practical life and have become very negative as a result.

Violet has a recognition of all things beautiful in her and she feels it very strongly, but she is beginning to become affected by her parents' attitudes and those of the other villagers. She is beginning to feel fear of the forest at night and of Old Mags. It is her own dreams which tell her to trust the two things she is being told she should not trust and through this she reaches her own intuitive self again and quietly goes about her life and fulfils her role. Then she waits until someone will listen and recognise herself. This is the turning inside which many people experience until they find that contact with themselves and can finally show their true selves and live without fear. But until the people in the village are ready to hear, she remains silent and quietly fulfils her purpose.

The importance of remembering old teaching

There was a legend which went back to the beginning of the history of the village and its founding parents. It followed a very clear message of living in harmony with the forest and never cutting the trees. They would give all that was needed. This is a theme that is prevalent throughout all major philosophies, belief systems and religions. The story demonstrates how important it is to be content with what you have and not want more. The majority of the village have rejected the legend as old rubbish, just a story and nothing more. They have closed their minds to its central wisdom because it no longer seems relevant to their modern lives. Progress must clear away all out-of-date attitudes. And so they listen to the new philosophies of materialism and the village loses its harmony. The wisdom within the old myth still held true in the present because it had a simple truth at heart: live in the harmony with yourself and your environment and all you need will be provided. The destruction of the forest symbolises the destruction felt by so many people whose lives have taken them away from the centre of contentment. Many young people are so desperate to have the latest designer label and parents struggle to find the money to provide it. The need to have things to make you feel good has subsumed the knowledge and teaching which tells us to be content with what we have and to believe in ourselves and what our inner truth tells us. Most people are so detached from their inner selves that they do not even believe there is this inner truth, yet those who take time to look inward will find it and the peace which goes with it. It is not necessary to be religious to experience this inner peace and contentment.

The importance of staying true to yourself and not following the majority

Violet and Old Mags did not get caught up in the enthusiasm of the village for the promises of the lumber company. Inside each of them there was the higher truth which made them circumspect and singled them both out for ridicule in different ways. Yet by sticking to their higher truths they were able to put things right. For some children who have such a sense of themselves and who are not listened to, it can be very lonely and isolating to live with their sense of isolation and yet they become unhappy if they try to conform. The pressure on everyone to conform is enormous and this story can help us to see that we should never give in because the truth will come through in the end. Both Violet and Mags are able to go above their fear and to stay close to their inner truths.

They have a firm set of beliefs and values in themselves which does not allow them to be swayed by anyone else. This is one of the most important assets for a successful life and yet it can seem pointless to fight against the majority. Many people will tell you that you are making life harder for yourself and you should just keep quiet and go along with things for an easy life. Life is not hard unless you fight it so although it might seem easier on the surface it will become harder in the end. The people in the village went along with what seemed like a good idea at the time, something to make life easier, and Violet has a really hard time of it. But in the end the whole village is faced by a much harder and potentially devastating problem which only Violet can put right. She had to stay quiet and carry out her work in silence, with the burden of ridicule upon her, but she was triumphant. The easy way is rarely the way to success in a whole sense. It may be a way of life which brings a veneer of success, but more is possible.

The importance of listening to children

Children who are not listened to are being denied their own truths. As adults, however simple or naive it may seem, whatever a child believes should be treated with respect. We are too quick in society to reject anything which might be demanding or challenging to our desire to live without responsibility, but in the end it will come back to us. Children mirror back to us that which we need to look at in ourselves. Violet mirrored back to her parents their dissatisfaction and greed and they did not like it, and so became angry with her. They rejected the message she tried to show them, they dismissed her and became unavailable to her. She turned to someone else for her inner guidance and development. To someone who did listen.

The abuse of power

This is a story of people who were given self-government and who forgot the important rules that went with it. They were given a shared power based on equality and respect for all that they had, including each other. Most of the people in the village had lived such a comfortable life that they had forgotten how to take decisions and had abdicated their responsibility to an outside influence. In many ways we do this through relationships. We make someone else responsible for our well-being and blame them when things go wrong. If a parent loses control and then blames the child for doing something to make them angry, they are abdicating responsibility for their own behaviour. If a child makes a mistake and is not helped to take responsibility for their actions in a loving, learning way, they will be unable to take responsibility for their own welfare and always blame someone else for their mistakes. Only Violet and Old Mags remain responsible for their own actions in the face of much obstruction and difficulty, thereby staying true to themselves and rescuing the others from their own misfortune, but in a way that obliges them to recognise and take responsibility for their mistakes. They allow Violet to guide them back to the intuitions which kept the truth alive.

Further Reading

Chosen Child Syndrome, The, Dr P. Love and J. Robinson, Piatkus Books.
Emotional Intelligence, Daniel Goleman, Bloomsbury.
Families and How to Survive Them, Skynner and Cleese, Mandarin Paperbacks.
Heart of Parenting, The, John Gottman and J. Declaire, Bloomsbury.
How to Talk so Kids will Listen and Listen so Kids will Talk, Faber and Mazlish, Avon Books (New York).
If it Hurts it Isn't Love, Spezzano Chuck, Hodder & Stoughton.
Love is Letting go of Fear, Gerald G. Jampolsky, Celestial Books (California).
That's Not What I Meant, Deborah Tannen, Virago.
When Parents Love Too Much, Ashner and Meyerson, Random Century.
Women Who Run With The Wolves, Clarissa Pinkola Estes, Rider Books/Random House.
You Just Don't Understand, Deborah Tannen, Virago.

Useful Contacts

Kidscape: (020) 7730 3300, Mon–Fri, 10 a.m.–4 p.m. For more information send s.a.e. to Kidscape, 152 Buckingham Palace Road, London SW1 9TR.
Childline: 0800 111 111, 24 hours a day.
Anti Bullying Campaign: (020) 7378 1446, Mon–Fri, 9.30 a.m.–5 p.m.

Most local health clinics and doctors surgeries have information about local youth counselling services or can put you in touch with family therapy teams and counsellors.

For details of one-day and weekend workshops for Personal Development run by the author, please contact Sylvia Clare on e-mail **sylvia.clare@btinternet.com** or visit the website on **http://www.btinternet.com/~sylvia.clare/**
or write to **Bowcombe Centre, Clattaford House, Clattaford Shute, Carisbrook, Isle of Wight PO30 1PD.**

Index